SNAPS, SCRAPS & SNIPPETS

of the Past and Present

How to Retrieve the Lost Pictures of Your Past

Lois J. Funk

RIT Publishing,
Central Illinois, U.S.A.

Copyright © 2014 Lois J. Funk

ISBN: 978-0-615-91303-2

Library of Congress Control Number: 2013919933

Limited edition. All rights reserved. No part of this publication may be reproduced or transmitted in any form or by any means, electronic or mechanical, including photocopying.

Cover design by Aubri L. Bacon
Cover Copyright © 2014 Aubri L. Bacon

Edited by Joan Johnson-Blackwell

Typesetting by Lois J. Funk

Printed in the United States of America

To all whose lives
have influenced mine...

ACKNOWLEDGEMENTS

"A Penny for Our Thoughts" *Peoria Poetry Club Bulletin,* 1994
"Apron Strings and Angel Wings" *Mother's Hands,* 1994; *Grandma's Hands,* 2005
"Aprons and Things" *Beatrice (Neb.) Daily Sun,* 2000
"Bringing in the Tree" *Peoria Poetry Club Bulletin,* 1993; *Touchstones of the Soul,* 1994
"Burned Up" *Beatrice (Neb.) Daily Sun,* 2002; *Father's Hands,* 2003
"Cinder Rocks and Hollyhocks" *Mother's Hands,* 1994; *Sisters,* 2003
"Dad's Sunday Shoes" *Father's Hands,* 2003
"Filling Mother's Shoes" *Mother's Hands,* 1994; *Beatrice (Neb.) Daily Sun,* 1998
"From Seedlings to 'Wheedlings'" *Sisters,* 2003
"Grandma and the Carousel" *Grandma's Hands,* 2005
"her recipe file" *Pieces of Her Mind,* 2012
"Highways from the Past" *Beatrice (Neb.) Daily Sun,* 2001; *Sisters,* 2003
"Leader of the Pack" *Father's Hands,* 2003
"Letter Overdue, Postmarked 1992" *Mother's Hands,* 1994; *Beatrice (Neb.) Daily Sun,* 2001
"Loads and Loads of Fun" *Sisters,* 2003
"More Highways from the Past" *Beatrice (Neb.) Daily Sun,* 2001; *Sisters,* 2003
"Mother's Hands" *Ideals Magazine,* 1989; *Peoria Journal Star,* 1989; *St. John's Lutheran Bulletin,* 1989; *Poets' Gold,* 1990; *The Silver Lining,* 1991; *Mother's Hands,* 1994; *Beatrice (Neb.) Daily Sun,* 1998; *Poems for Mother,* 2000
"No Special Day" *Beatrice (Neb.) Daily Sun,* 2002
Omar Bakery, Milwaukee, Wisconsin (about 1939-1960)
"Pass the Onions, Please!" *Grandma's Hands,* 2005
""Plum" Crazy" *Father's Hands,* 2003
"Refinishing the Piano" *Climbing the Woost Family Tree,* 2002
"Sipping Memories" *Beatrice (Neb.) Daily Sun,* 2004; *Mother's Hands II,* 2003
"The Button Jar" *Mother's Hands II,* 2003
"The Hang-Ups of 'Quality' Time" *Mother's Hands,* 1994; *Beatrice (Neb.) Daily Sun,* 1999
"The Old Gray Plymouth" *Father's Hands,* 2003
"The Sprinter" *Touchstones of the Soul,* 1994
"The Thorn in Grandpa's Backside" *Beatrice (Neb.) Daily Sun,* 2000; *Grandma's Hands,* 2005
"Under Grandma's Spell" *Grandma's Hands,* 2005
"Watered-Down Bargains" *Mother's Hands,* 1994; *Beatrice (Neb.) Daily Sun,* 1999

SNAPS, SCRAPS & SNIPPETS

of the Past and Present

How to Retrieve the Lost Pictures of Your Past

Endorsements

In *Snaps, Scraps and Snippets,* Lois Funk provides writers young and not-so-young with practical tools to help them re-discover lost memories and find fresh inspiration in them. She shows through her own personal experiences how using these tools can make anyone a better writer. After all, any life can be turned into an exciting story if you are a good storyteller. — **Kevin Kizer, Sr. Writer,** *The Peorian* **magazine**

Too often beginning writers are told to "show, not tell." However, they are not told how to do that. Lois Funk, in *Snaps, Scraps, and Snippets* uses the example of taking pictures and vignettes from her childhood and trips abroad to do exactly that. Every beginning writer (and some seasoned ones) should read this book. It is charming and endearing and uses the simplest of things — such as a sieve — to show one how to sort through the good and bad of one's writing. I would definitely recommend this book for my beginning students. — **Alvin Thomas Ethington, Editor,** *Pieces of Her Mind;* **staged playwright, published author, and professional reviewer.**

CONTENTS

Dedication	iii
Acknowledgements	iv
Introduction - Marching to the Beat	1
Part I - Looking Through the Viewfinder	
Chapter 1 - Getting the Idea	7
Chapter 2 - Trash or Treasure?	11
Chapter 3 - Getting Motivated: The Three Ds	15
Chapter 4 - Dusting Off the Camera	31
Chapter 5 - Preparing the Darkroom	45
Part II - Finding the Focus	
Chapter 1 - Unlocking the Past	53
Chapter 2 - Digging Up the Bones	61
Chapter 3 - Poking Around the Cellar	71
Chapter 4 - Walking Back Through Time	105
Chapter 5 - Taking Shortcuts	121
Chapter 6 - Exploring the Waters	137
Chapter 7 - Sifting Through the Sand	175
Chapter 8 - Putting Time through a Sieve	159

Part III - Using a Wide-Angle Lens

    Chapter 1 - Moving Toward the Window   197

    Chapter 2 - Putting the Past in Perspective   207

Conclusion - Getting to the End of the Roll   211

Introduction

Marching to the Beat

Imagine, for a moment, that you have just given a child his first traditional (versus digital) camera, complete with several rolls of film. Imagine, too, that the child already knows how to look through the viewfinder and how to push the button that releases the shutter and snaps the picture. What he *doesn't* know is how to find good subjects to photograph. So, after wasting several rolls of film on meaningless objects that no one else cares to look at, he comes back to you. Now he asks how to find subjects that others may want to see, simply because the subjects are so different, or so similar, to what they know.

You could *tell* the child that there is a process called trial and error and that he'll learn, as time goes by, what types of subjects make good pictures. *Or* you could pick up the camera and say, "Like this," as you click a close-up of the questioning look on his face. Of course, *showing* is much more effective than *telling*, and that's exactly what I hope to do in this book — to show, rather than tell, how anyone short of having a diagnosed memory problem can find good writing materials for their personal journals and/or memoirs.

This book is merely one more attempt to answer the age-old questions posed by every would-be writer who actually wants to put pen to paper: *Where do you get your ideas?* or *How do you find so many things to write about?* Either of which might be interpreted as *Show me how you do it so that I can do it too.* Enter, the beat of the "show, don't tell" drum that sets the tone and synchronizes the steps of writers who've learned that anything short of *showing* how to find things to write about leaves would-be writers hanging from the threads of their next thoughts: *that they don't have any interesting experiences to write about; or that they can't remember enough of their past to write about it.* On the contrary, I believe that even children who have lived in this world and are capable of reading and writing have something to write about, if not for the whole world to read, at least for their own satisfaction and as a way of preserving whatever history they have experienced. Their only problem lies in thinking that *their* experiences don't count.

My husband and I had a dear poet friend (a poet buddy, we called him) who had experienced a whopping measure of history, including years of military service during World War II. But, although he wrote beautiful Edgar Guest type poetry that everyone loved and waited to hear, he rarely read one of his poems aloud without apologizing for it first, even as he was making his way to the microphone. I often gave him a friendly scolding for putting himself and his poetry down.

When he claimed that he had nothing more to write about, I could only imagine the oodles of childhood memories and wartime experiences that he *wasn't* writing about. And sure enough, when he died unexpectedly, those of us who had heard him speak so modestly of himself and his poetry were shocked to find that he had received several military medals, including the Purple Heart.

We all have memories that are too painful to write about, simply because we can't distance ourselves from them. Until we can, those memories are best left alone. However, for those of you who *do* want to write about past experiences but think you've already lost too many memories to make that possible, or that you have little or nothing interesting to write about, my goal is to show that some (or most) of your memories may not be lost at all.

They may just be waiting for you to reveal their hiding places, to bring them out into the light and record them in any way you see fit.

The *Getting the Picture* exercises throughout this book are aimed at doing just that—literally getting you up out of your chair to search for forgotten memories because, whether you draw from the past, concentrate on the present, or dream about the future, there are memories out there to write about. The challenge lies in *finding* those that have, until now, been lying just beyond your reach, in some secret corner of your mind; in dragging them out into the open, kicking and screaming, if necessary; and in preserving them to the best of your ability. As you're about to see, memories *do* hide in all sorts of places....

As an added incentive, you may want to consider reserving a special binder for your *Getting the Picture* exercises.

Part I

Looking Through the Viewfinder

Chapter 1

Getting the Idea

Few people would deny that the past, good or bad, is best preserved through pictures, whether they are printed photographs that can be touched and held and ogled over, or printed word pictures (the kind this book deals with) that can be touched, held, and read.

Many of us cling to scads of photographs of one kind or another, storing them in boxes or albums, on our walls, or in our wallets. But, unlike those tangible photographs of the past that we *consciously* hide from the elements of dust and moisture and fingerprints, we tend to keep our *mental* pictures, or images of the past, *sub*consciously hidden away, sometimes so deeply that we fail to develop them.

In fact, we have a tendency to think that the greater share of the images locked away in the nooks and crannies of our minds can never be retrieved. But I have found that a good many of them can be pried loose and coaxed into the present, with the use of three special tools I call *snaps*, *scraps*, and *snippets*.

In my quest to bring back my past and write about it, I find that I can, to some degree at least, reverse the picture/memory process of using *tangible* photographs to record the past. To reverse the process, I simply use whatever details I remember about the past to conjure up additional *mental* pictures, or images, that have been lost to years of neglect — not intentional neglect on my part, but the natural letting go, or fading away, of memories as years go by. When the details of those past events — details I need, to make my writing come alive — seem just beyond my grasp, I reach for one or more of those special tools: *snaps* (tangible *snaps*hots or photographs that I may already have, plus the mental images that I keep getting and developing along the way); *scraps* (bits and pieces of tangible or remembered items, from trivial trinkets to priceless heirlooms); and *snippets* (small but important details I've learned to glean from all sorts of places).

Once a few of those buried images are brought out into the open, I develop them into what I call word pictures. Sometimes the word pictures are detailed, written descriptions, i.e. biographical stories, which I immediately add to my journal; sometimes they are merely lists of images that I recall and add to my journal as such. Regardless of their size or content, once the word pictures are on paper, I use them to create poems. Those poems, along with my journal, are my way of preserving my memories, in fact, of recording my life story.

For skeptics who claim they've already lost too many memories of the past to find them, let alone write about them, I can only say that I thought the same thing until I learned how to reverse the picture/memory process, and how to put *snaps*, *scraps*, and *snippets* to work for me.

To my surprise, when I first decided to write about my past, the more seemingly-insignificant memories I consciously tugged at, thought about, and wrote about, no matter how small, the more mental images of my childhood came to mind. It was like walking down a long corridor, opening one door after another and finding something new and exciting to write about behind each one. And I'm still walking and still finding doors to open.

Now I hope to show those of you who want to delve into *your* pasts — to walk the corridor and open the doors — how to find at least *some* of your lost or elusive memories through the use of *snaps*, *scraps*, and *snippets*. Of course, not all writings, poems or otherwise, will require the use of all three tools, so it will be up to you to determine which tools will or will not work for you.

What you do with any portion of the *snaps*, *scraps*, and/or *snippets* you gather along the way, or how you want to write about them, is also entirely up to you. I simply hope to help you *find* your lost memories through the use of tools that work for me and to show that, once you begin the developing process, even the faintest images have an uncanny way of coaxing additional ones to surface. As proof, I offer a few such details that made their way into my mind's camera, and into this book, even as I was proofing the final draft. Those details, which came about through the use of *snaps*, *scraps* and *snippets*, are indicated by *(sss)* and are further explained in the text box below the revised paragraph or at the end of that section.

Chapter 2

Trash or Treasure?

I have an old-fashioned scrapbook—the kind with browning manila pages, which I bought with my saved-up allowance when I was about ten years old. I only glance through it occasionally, usually when I'm shifting it from one storage spot to another. I can't bear to throw it away *or* to transfer its contents (most of which have forever lain loose between its pages) to a more up-to-date, contemporary scrapbook, because either option would mean discarding a bit of my past.

Even as I retrieved the scrapbook last night, hoping to find something useful in the way of writing this book, I expected to find its contents ordinary and insignificant. Instead, the distance of several decades gave me a closer look at myself as others must have seen me during my growing-up years. It was like pulling up behind a car or a van with stickers plastered all over its backside. We've all seen them, either arranged in neat little rows on the back window or bumper, or slapped helter-skelter onto the car's finish: souvenir stickers from holiday resorts, confessions of religious beliefs (or lack of them), pledges of patriotism, campaign stickers still supporting the last loser in the Presidential race. Whatever the stickers promote, advertise, or criticize, the combination of them all generally reveals the character of the vehicle's owner(s).

Within the manila pages of my scrapbook, my pre and early teen years are summarized by diplomas and certificates for Vacation Bible School and Junior Reading Circle; a 3" x 5" registration/class schedule that I filled out for seventh grade, on which I proudly entered my father's occupation as "Occupant of Caterpillar"; a watercolor birthday cake on a loose sheet of manila paper whose edges have darkened with age; a newspaper clipping and an official looking index card acknowledging a fellow seventh-grader and myself as first place winners in the Halloween Downtown (Pekin, Illinois) Window Painting Contest of 1955; a note from my English teacher encouraging me to look at my audience when I talk; and two school library notices of overdue books, one of which was *The Gay Poet*.

That I was interested in poetry as a teenager shouldn't have been a surprise. The same English teacher who told me to look at my audience when I spoke also wrote in my autograph book, "I shall expect to see your name in magazines someday as a writer." Her expectations were met in 1981, when I sent her several issues of *Children's Playmate* and *Turtle Magazine* (Children's Better Health Institute, The Benjamin Franklin Literary & Medical Society, Inc.) containing poems and stories with my byline.

The newspaper article and index card took me back to Court Street, in downtown Pekin, Illinois, on Halloween day, 1955, where ninety-two merchants allowed twice that many area students to paint Halloween scenes on their storefront windows. My girlfriend and I arrived early that morning, at the plate glass display window of Carps department store, with our detailed sketch of a typical Halloween scene in hand — haunted house; witch on broom; gnarled tree; and black cat — to ready our water paints and brushes for the precise moment when we would be told to begin. It took us the better part of the day to outline the scene and fill it in, as curious shoppers geared down to slow motion, dodging us and our paints while nodding their approval, and judges skulked around, comparing gaudy paintings that lined the sidewalks of the main street. After the judging, our "masterpieces" remained on the storefronts for a few days before being washed into gutters and storm sewers.

The watercolor birthday cake, along with my class schedule, puts me in my seventh grade art class, at Pekin's Edison Jr. High School, Room 41, Period 3, in a middle desk that I occupied on February 22nd (and on every school day of 1955), from 10:46 to 11:46 a.m. On that particular day, the teacher left us to our drawings while he busied himself at his desk. The next thing we knew, he was handing me the still-wet watercolor of a pink birthday cake, complete with thirteen flaming candles. The significance of that painting grew all the more precious this week, when I unexpectedly caught sight of that teacher's name and death date on a tombstone in a local cemetery.

Now, the question is, will any one of these items, and the story behind it, or any other *scraps* that I've saved and written about through the years, be of any interest to my descendants? Perhaps no more than my parents' and grandparents' stories about how far they walked to school in knee-deep snow held my attention once I'd grown weary of the tales. Could the answer, therefore, lie not only in how much of my past I can recall, but also in how the stories are told; and in whether or not I can turn them into colorful word pictures and poems that readers can *see* and *feel* and *experience* for themselves? Hopefully so, and *if* so, then *maybe* my stories will be treasured rather than trashed in years to come.

Several years ago, I set a goal of creating a different kind of scrapbook. It would be a memoir, of sorts, but instead of manila or magnetic pages that hold tangible mementos, it would be a book of written descriptions that would bring the echoes of the past reverberating into the present. I chose to write those descriptions in poetic form, ignoring stern warnings that poetry—especially the traditional style, with rhyme and meter—was no longer favored by readers or publishers. However, I did read once, and *only* once, that if you can do it well (the rhyme and rhythm), it's worth a try. Attestation that traditional poetry *is* still acceptable to some publishers and a good many readers lies in the collection of books and magazines that contain my byline.

That memoirs should probably not be written in poetic form, or that we should not attempt to cover an entire lifetime in one book, might be another arguable point for some, but not for me. Proof that poetic memoirs work lies in a collection of poetry that I edited and typeset for the widow of our poet buddy. When she handed me a folder of his 250 plus poems, I set to work putting them in chronological order, from his earliest memories to his anticipated requiem. Sometime after the book was printed, his widow called to say that her husband's brother had read the book from beginning to end seven times, reliving *his own* childhood, and much of his own life, with every reading.

My greatest fear of writing my own stories was that I wouldn't be able to recall enough details to make them interesting for someone else to read. But as one remembered thought led to another, and as I found various ways of unlocking the past, readers of my poems seemed to "sink into" them, simply because they recognized and related to situations the poems described. Readers unknowingly give the greatest of all compliments when tears well up in their eyes and they say something like, *That reminds me of...* or *I remember doing that!* Now, besides showing others how to find their hidden memories the way I'm still finding mine, I hope to show that *any* memory, good or bad, can be turned into one or more word pictures, poems, or essays that the average reader can sink into and enjoy reading.

Chapter 3

Getting Motivated: The Three *D*s

Motivation is fueled by *d*esire, guided by *d*esign, and driven by *d*etermination. It is, in turn, nurtured by all three.

Desire motivates me to write about and share my past, not because it was so *different* from everyone else's, but because it was so *like* everyone else's. People enjoy reading what they can relate to, in this case, poems about *things* (items they remember their parents or themselves using) and *situations* they are familiar with, perhaps because of similar incidents in their own lives, perhaps because of incidents that could, or should, have been. It isn't unusual for such poems to pull comments like, "I've often had the same thoughts but just wouldn't know how to go about putting them on paper."

While the majority of my poems are inspired by feelings and situations that are uniquely my own, I cannot honestly say that they pertain only to me, or to my life. They are about anyone and everyone who has ever had similar experiences. As such, they allow readers to become the main characters and relive the moments for themselves. In a sense, then, writing a poem is like painting a picture for someone else to "step into."

That 'stepping-into' privilege became mine the first time I read Edgar Guest's "The Furnace Door" (from the *Collected Verse of Edgar A. Guest*, Contemporary Books, Inc.). That poem took me back to my own childhood, to the point that I could actually hear the creaking and clanking of *our* furnace door, the scraping of *my* dad's coal scoop on the concrete floor of our coal bin, the quick thrusting and pulling back, and the coal sliding off the scoop as it flew into the furnace. In short, it could have been my own father in that poem.

Design, or intent, guides me to the notion that I want to leave my descendants something of my life that might touch theirs, solely because it pertains to, and includes, them. As a genealogist, tracing my family tree has taught me, both as researcher and descendant, not to be satisfied with flat, boring, pages of names, dates and events that merely fill a book with a family name printed on its cover. Other than finding a lost or elusive relative, one of the greatest rewards of compiling a family tree is to come across a photograph and/or a tangible memento of an ancestor whose lifelong profession or reputation has already piqued my curiosity. And, better yet, or at least comparable to finding a photograph, is to discover a written tribute, a character sketch that tells me something *in depth* about that person.

Photographs *show*, words *tell* — *or* so it would seem. But sometimes the opposite is true, especially when it comes to describing a person's character. A photograph might *tell* us exactly what an ancestor *looked* like, while leaving his character as flat as a tintype. Words, on the other hand, can *show* us who he was by describing, in detail, not only his nature, but his accomplishments and mannerisms, as well as his likes and dislikes. Along with photographs *and* description, tangible mementos become welcome extras that help to clarify and deepen our appreciation of the past, thus making us aware that the character or ancestor in question has definitely touched a part of our lives.

Putting Snaps, Scraps, *and* Snippets *to Work*

- Using *Snaps,* Old or New

With my mother's help, I found a black and white *snap*shot of my paternal grandfather, which told me that he was tall and gaunt, yet, because he died before I was born, I had no idea what he was really like. Still, I had a driving desire to write *something* about him. In order to do that, I needed to go beyond *snaps,* to find something tangible that he had owned or used, or that had been a part of his life. That's when I started looking for *scraps*—not scraps as in leftover waste to be discarded, but scraps in the sense of being the only part left of something we would like to have back or, at least, to see.

- Finding *Scraps* Wherever They Lie

Again, the only available *scraps* that pertained to my grandfather came from things my mother saved after my father died, and from my uncle (my dad's brother): a crude wooden chain with unbroken, moveable links that my grandfather had whittled from one piece of wood; a set of needles in a leather pouch that he had used for making and mending fishing nets; and a special tool for removing a swallowed hook from a fish's stomach. But even those weren't enough to tell me what my grandfather was really like. Thus it was time to turn to *snippets* of information gleaned from conversations with neighbors who had known him, and from relatives—some whose reluctance to talk about my grandfather would give me even more determination to write about him.

- Gleaning *Snippets* Along the Way

I had always known that my grandfather was a building contractor and that he had died of tuberculosis before I was born. What I had paid little attention to was the fact that he also owned a small riverboat that he used for commercial fishing and hunting, and that he kept that boat moored somewhere along the riverbank at the foot of town. But I couldn't stop there.

Through conversations with those who knew him, I found that he also had a small shack on the river; that he spent many nights either in that shack or on the riverboat, with little or no heat to fight the dampness; that the fishing nets and decoys that had hung in our basement for years (and that I had somewhat ignored) had belonged to him; that he always took the boat downriver in the fall, to hunt and fish; and that his brothers, at least, had visited him and eaten meals he had prepared for them on that boat.

My next step was to write a detailed word picture for my journal. Then I was able to come up with a poem that best describes my grandfather and his life as I see it.

Grandpa Simon

You sleep beside her *now*, unaware of
the chill that penetrates your bones.
You wasted away before I was born,
your soul threatened by consumption
long before your body ever was, though
your children would never admit
you spent little time at home,
opting instead for a riverside shack at
the foot of town, with a
riverboat whose planked hull
soaked up no small portion of the
river itself and whose decks were
forever drenched with
nets of hauled-in fish.

Come autumn, you'd
make your way downriver to
sleep in dank darkness and
live off the bounty of
your hunting skills.
Your brother, at a century's age, still
marveled at your eagerness to serve up
feasts of mallards for visitors to
your floating domain.

When you took sick, Dad went to
collect the cumbersome nets and

strings of hand-carved decoys from
your boat in the slough; brought them home
to hang from basement rafters, alongside
his own waders, in the house you built
before he was born.

In summary, the *snap*shot of my grandfather showed me how tall and gaunt (and far from healthy looking) he was; the *scraps* were instrumental in setting the mood for what I wanted and needed, to write about him; and the *snippets* helped me fill in the blanks. In addition, the leftover *scraps* and *snippets* will eventually become the subjects of other poems.

❖ Getting the Picture
Find a *snap*shot of a late ancestor and place it in front of you. If you don't have such a photograph, consider going to an antique mall and finding one of someone else's ancestor. From whatever images come to mind, write a detailed word picture (description) of what you see — the hairdo, the dress, the expression in the eyes, or on the lips, and even what you imagine that person might be thinking. Then write anything you remember, or have heard, about the life and character of that person. Your notes could include details about his work, his hobbies, where he lived, etc. Include any real or imagined recollections of sound, touch, or smell, being as truthful as you dare while

remembering that the rough draft should be for your eyes only. If the subject in the photo is someone you never met and know nothing about, use your imagination to come up with a fictional word picture. Once you have all the details written down and/or transferred to your journal, use them to write a poem or an essay about the person in the photograph.

Determination keeps me searching through the past, groping for images that eventually evolve, or develop, into word pictures for readers to *see*. But what if all the *snaps, scraps* and *snippets* I can gather are still not enough to let me write about a particular person or event as thoroughly as I'd like to? In order to bring back details that have all but slipped away, I turn to what I have dubbed "guided" freewriting.

Teachers have long been using freewriting to help students who can't put their thoughts on paper for one reason or another. Similarly, writers use it to break through writer's block.

*Free*writing is every bit as *free* and *freeing as* its name suggests. While it requires only pen and paper, it encourages the mind to run wild and *free* with no boundaries other than the edges of the paper and the supply of ink. As a result, hand and pen move *free*ly across the page, mysteriously *free*ing up thoughts that are buried somewhere in the subconscious.

The process is simple: write nonstop for ten minutes or so, about anything, about nothing, about whatever comes to mind (even if the "whatever" turns out to be utter nonsense), and sooner or later something worth using is bound to surface.

While I am a true advocate of freewriting in general, I balk at the thought of wasting time writing about nothing when I want only to get some substantial details on paper; hence the need for *guided* freewriting—writing nonstop for as long as it takes about a *particular* subject that has already caught my attention.

When I sat down to write a poem about my very first day of school, I had no *snaps* or *scraps* to inspire me, and all of the *snippets* I could come up with weren't enough to put me back in my first grade room long enough to let me capture the details. The solution? A *guided* freewriting session—writing nonstop until I had exhausted the details of that day.

The result of that free-writing session follows. Grammar and punctuation have been left uncorrected; additions made for the sake of clarity are enclosed in [brackets]. Once I had finished the session, I copied the notes into my journal. That journal entry eventually became the basis, and the inspiration, for a poem entitled "The Doorway to Change."

Journal Entry: First Day, First Grade

"I didn't want Mom to leave me there. I don't remember looking forward to going to school or being anxious to get there, although I probably was. We walked that day, [probably] with my sister, who was already in the third grade by that time, but I don't remember the walk. I just remember standing in the open door of my first grade room—the auditorium of Lincoln School, on State Street, in Pekin, Illinois—and the teacher, Miss G, coming to the door to speak to me and talk to Mom.

I remember the openness of the room, the hugeness of it, with the stage at the front and a theatrical-type maroon curtain with gold braiding and a large gold "L" in the center. I remember the tables—rectangular ones with chairs my size—near the foot of the stage, not lined up, but arranged in such a way that Miss G could circle the entire group in a matter of seconds, it seemed; and the large expanse of open hardwood floor that I had to walk across to get to them.

I stood frozen in that doorway, and the next thing I knew, Mom had disappeared. I had never been with total strangers before, except when I got lost at the carnival, and now here I was, with a whole roomful of kids I didn't know and a teacher that had the nervous habit of opening and closing her lips (like the bass Dad caught up North) without actually opening her mouth or separating her teeth. And now I had to make that long walk with her, across the hardwood floor. I felt like everyone was staring at me, and I thought it strange that no one else seemed to mind being there.

There must have been six or eight rectangular tables (or maybe there were only four) with chairs on each side. My chair faced the stage. I sat with three other girls. Miss G continually walked around the tables, talking, looking, asking questions. I didn't answer any of them. Then she gave us pencils and paper—the manila kind that had widely spaced blue or green lines with red lines in between so that you could learn how high to make capital letters and how short to make small ones—and asked us to write our numbers, 1 through 9. No problem. Mom had taught me those. (Kindergarten was an "option" that Mom and Dad didn't opt for.)

Miss G was quietly slipping around the tables, looking, *spying.* I wrote my numbers neatly—hiding my paper with my left hand and letting my hair fall down onto the paper so that no one could see it—and felt quite confident, until I realized that I was done long before the others. That worried me. Had I done it right? Why were the others taking so long? Then came the shock. I looked at the other girls' papers. Their numbers weren't like mine! My "2" had a loop, and my "three" had a curve at the top instead of a straight line, and my "four" was open at the top, and my "8" was a continuous figure 8 line instead of the snowman-like circles stacked on top of each other like theirs. *How could Mom have taught me wrong?* What would the teacher say? She was slipping my way! I just wouldn't let her see. I kept my hand and my hair over my paper. But there she was, standing right over me, *demanding* to see my paper.

My face was burning, my hands sweating. I lifted my head a little and slid my hand and arm off my paper, but she still had to bend over to see. She smiled and went on! Whew! I guessed it was okay after all.

Lincoln School had two floors: 1-3 grades on first, 4-6 grades on second; two rooms of each grade, one of each on each side of the building. The basement housed the gym and the restrooms. The girls' restroom [which had no doors whatsoever on the stalls] was patrolled [during recess] by Miss G, who insisted we "go" whether we had to or not; and even if I had to, I didn't, although I pretended I did just to satisfy her."

While my guided freewriting notes contain only thoughts and images about that particular day, they are dotted with *I don't remember*s, *probably*s, and *maybe*s. The fact that I didn't actually remember some things, like whether or not my sister walked with Mom and me, didn't stop me from saying that she probably did, simply because I knew we were always side by side. But the mere suggestion of those unclear images coaxed more and more realizations to surface — the hardwood floor of the auditorium, for instance; which way my chair faced; and how many kids were sitting at my table. Those were not things I had consciously thought about *before* the guided freewriting session.

The Doorway to Change

I stand frozen in the moment,
betrayed by a mother who led me
right up to the door and
disappeared the second
my back was turned,
leaving me with a stranger who
wants to escort me across
a large expanse of hardwood floor,
to tables teeming with
kids I don't know.

She did not tell me
this moment would come;
that she'd not be staying;

that fear might take over;
or that I'd be spending my days
with someone other than her.
So all I know for sure is that
I am not ready
for this thing they call
school.

❖ Getting the Picture

Think of a subject, a day, or a particular event that you've always wanted to write about but couldn't come up with enough details to do so. Then, with pen in hand, and plenty of paper, sit down for an uninterrupted session of *guided* freewriting, channeling all of your thoughts to that particular subject, day, or event. If you can't remember what it was *truly* like, write what it was *probably* like, or what it *could* or *should have been* like. And if, in the process, a true image flows into your mind and onto your paper, circle it quickly and go on. If you're still writing freely after a page or two, don't stop. Keep writing and keep circling.

When you are satisfied that you have recorded every detail you can think of, copy the most telling *snippets* (especially the circled ones) into your journal for future use, or use them immediately to write a poem or an essay. But don't be surprised if, later in the day—or in the middle of the night—additional images crop up, demanding to be recorded.

Chapter 4

Dusting Off the Camera

Ask a child to create a scrapbook without the benefit of photographs or tangible mementos, and he will surely rely on memory to conjure up pictures of his favorite things, making them real and touchable (at least to him) by drawing or writing them on paper. Our challenge, as writers wanting to record our own thoughts and feelings about our pasts, is to do the same thing. But unlike children, who are closer in time to everything they'll record, we sometimes have to draw on memories that have been tucked away for so long that we first have to find them. In other words, we have to "get the picture" before we can write about it.

Photographs, no matter how precious, tend to get lost or buried or tossed away. Similarly, memories that have the potential to become good word pictures (highly detailed, written descriptions), or ideas for writing, get lost in the shuffle of busy schedules, buried beneath the debris of other thoughts, or tossed away, that is, given up as being too trivial to think about, let alone write about. In order to draw those memories back to the surface, the writer needs to drag out the mind's camera, dust it off, and start getting some good images that can be developed into word pictures and then turned into meaningful poems or essays. Dusting off the camera might be compared to "getting the cobwebs out of our brains," as our teachers used to say, so that we can observe what's been stored there and is just waiting to be retrieved. Although some details of the past may be temporarily out of sight, it doesn't mean that they are lost forever. There *are* ways of bringing them back to mind, and photographs, or *snaps*, are just one of those ways.

On my ninth Christmas, I received a Kodak Baby Brownie Special and a few rolls of film, after which I became responsible for paying for my own film and processing. I soon learned to shoot wisely in order to avoid wasting film. Still, I looked diligently for interesting subjects to photograph, and when there didn't seem to be any, resorted to taking seemingly dull shots of home, church, and school. Dull, I thought, until recently, when the details in some of those pictures jogged my memory and gave me some unexpected writing material. One example that comes instantly to mind is a black and white photo taken by a teacher, of my third grade class at Lincoln School, in Pekin, Illinois.

It wasn't the *Why are you taking this picture?* look on some of our faces that caught my attention but, rather, the background: a wide, brick stairway attached to a back corner of the school, on the girls' yard side of the building, with pipe railings running up each side and a thick concrete landing at the top. The steps led to double steel doors that seldom, if ever, were opened. So no one minded that, every recess, my girlfriends and I climbed the steps and took claim to the landing in front of those doors, to resume the girl talk that had been cut short with the previous return-to-your-room bell. From that photo, then, I immediately made a journal entry (word picture) that covered ideas for at least two more childhood poems — one about the brick stairway and landing, and one about those recess talks.

It was during my Kodak Brownie years that I learned to carry a camera most everywhere I went, a habit that still has me grabbing one or more newer models from the closet for any special occasion. (The Brownie was retired in 1967, when an emaciated cow in Banaris, India, kicked it from my husband's hand and sent it flying through the air.)

While a large percentage of the photographs I take are close-ups, mainly because I am more interested in the color of a person's eyes than in the shoes they are wearing, my search for childhood memories taught me a valuable lesson about the pictures, written and otherwise, that I want to leave for my descendants. Designers of today's scrapbook kits advise us to sort through our photographs, get rid of the bad ones, and give (or throw) away any duplicates. Then we're to take the good ones, cut away the backgrounds, and put what's left in the scrapbook. Had I followed those instructions with the picture of my classmates at Lincoln School, I *would not have* a picture of the brick stairway that led to the unused doors, that was so much a part of those days, and that inspires me to want to write about it.

When I started refinishing the 1929 Richmond upright piano my husband and I had scavenged from an old farm house, I rummaged through several black and white pictures my mother had given me, searching for ones I remembered seeing, of my great-grandparents sitting side by side in front of the upright piano in *their* parlor. Although I had formerly been interested only in their faces, I now wanted to see what the *piano* itself looked like and, more importantly, what was sitting *on top of it*.

I scrutinized the photos with a magnifying glass, taking in the lace runner; the oval picture frames that held faces I didn't recognize; and the open sheet music on the music stand that stood beside the piano; but searching most of all for a glimpse of the metronome my mother had used during music lessons at her grandmother's — *this* grand-mother's — house. While Mom's memories of those lessons *and* her grandmother were very unpleasant ones, they tugged at my desire to get them down on paper, so much so that as I continued to remove the rock-hard, blackened varnish from my piano, scenes of my great-grandparents' era, as I imagined them, set my mind's camera whirling with images and word pictures for a poem that eventually surfaced along with the beautiful cherry finish of the Richmond.

Refinishing the Piano

A relic of someone else's past,
it revels in its own unmasking,
its delicate features, rich and red,
taking center stage now, parting
layers of time-worn curtains to
let me slip, unseen, through tapestried
parlors reeking of cigars and

oldness; to let me breathe in the
familiar air of uncharted notes falling
deftly into place, only to stop short
with the *crack!* of the wooden pointer
on Mother's tender knuckles while
the metronome keeps time with
my heartbeat.

Although none of what I'd gleaned from the old photograph (the lace runner, the oval picture frames, the music, or the music stand) actually appears in the finished poem, each and every item played an important part in setting the mood of the poem. That mood helped me reach the point I wanted to get across: that my mother, who had the God-given talent for playing by ear, was sharply reprimanded by her grandmother/music teacher for adding fill-in notes to pieces as she played.

The refinishing incident spurred me on, and I anxiously searched through my childhood photo album to find the deep-down pictures of our home life. But I was disappointed to find that pictures don't really lie; they just don't always tell the whole truth, and the little things I so desperately wanted to see didn't show up in the photos.

I wanted to see the cinder driveway that had once run alongside our house, and the garbage pits and hollyhocks that had lined the alley behind it. I longed to see pictures of Mom's clotheslines propped up and loaded down with the week's wash; the tricycle that my sisters and I took turns riding to the neighborhood park just up the street from our house; and glimpses of my grandma's kitchen where, in the aprons my mother always made for her, she taught me how to spell my name while she was baking cherry pies. Those were the details that added color and life to my childhood. But nowhere did I find them recorded on film. So I did the next best thing. I encouraged my mind's camera to come up with mental images that I could translate onto paper, using word pictures *in place of* tangible photographs that I couldn't find. My patience paid off when I was finally able to bring familiar scenes back to life by writing those word pictures and then shaping them into poems, not only for myself, but for others to relate to as well. The word pictures themselves always become a part of my journal.

Journal Entry: Mom's Washday (revised)

"Mom always did the family wash on Mondays, rain or shine, because every other day of the week was reserved for other jobs: Tuesday, ironing; Wednesday, cleaning at Grandma's; Thursday, sewing and miscellaneous; Friday, cleaning at home.

On fair and even cold washdays, Mom would hang the clothes outside, on wire lines (that had to be wiped clean of dirt and rust and dew), and prop them up so that the longer pieces wouldn't drag on the ground when the wires stretched under the weight of wet blue jeans and shirts and sheets. But on washdays threatened by dark skies, she'd hang them on heavy cord lines that Dad had strung from hooks, along the lengths of our basement rafters.

In winter, the furnace heat helped dry the clothes in no time at all. But in summer, when the humidity was so high that it dripped from the water pipes, she'd unlock the square, double-paned windows that hinged at the top, and swing them inward and up, where their hooks fastened to eyes screwed into the rafters. On those days, the basement air grew heavy with the *Dreft*-fresh smell of wet cotton and denim.

Washing was an all-day job back then. First, the wringer washer and rinse tubs had to be wheeled out into the center of the basement, near the floor drain, and filled. Since the water was used for more than one load, the white, less dirty clothes always went in first. Then the agitator was set in motion by manually moving a lever on the outside of the machine *(sss)*. When Mom was satisfied that the clothes were clean, she'd turn off the agitator; put the clothes through the wringer a piece or two at a time, letting them curl flatly into the first rinse tub, where she'd swirl them around by hand; then transfer them, via the wringer, into the second tub, for a final rinse. She'd put them back through the wringer at least once, and maybe twice, before letting them curl on through and drop into a bushel basket with an oil-cloth-type lining that kept the basket material from bleeding onto the damp clothes. Once the basket was full, she'd carry it outside, where I'd help her hang the clothes while the next load was agitating.

> *(sss)* While revising my washday journal entry for this book, I suddenly realized that I didn't remember *how* Mom got the wringer washer to agitate. I was about to call my sister, who had purchased a wringer washer just for the fun of having one, when a clear laundry-day image washed into my mind's camera—that of Mom pushing or pulling an arm, or lever, on the outside of the washer, to start or stop the agitator. Later confirmation by my sister gave proof that the use of *snaps, scraps and snippets* really does work.

Throughout the morning, Mom (or I) would make extra trips up the stairs, to the lines outside, checking to see if any clothes were dry enough to take down so that we could make room for more.

Most of the clothes ended up being very stiff, especially when there was no wind to whip them dry. So once we took them down, we left them in the baskets, ready for sprinkling and ironing come Tuesday morning."

Poems derived from word pictures and/or journal entries, like the one above, have become a part of my ongoing memoirs:

The Hang-Ups of 'Quality' Time

I like to hang my clothes out on
The line, like Mother did
Back in the days when moms stayed home
And I was just a kid;
When Monday was the day reserved
For washing, rain or shine,
And no one dared burn garbage once
The clothes were on the line.

Mom's washday started just as soon
As Dad was on the road;
She'd wheel the wringer washer out
And start the first white load.
I'd sit down on the basement stairs
To watch her, as a rule,
While both my sisters finished getting
Dressed to go to school.
She'd have a basket heaping by
The time they both were gone,
And I'd be right behind her, traipsing
Through the dew-drenched lawn;

For clotheslines have a way of holding
On to dew and dust,
And it was I who got to wipe
Those lines of last week's rust.
While Mom hung blouses, dresses, shirts,
And skirts that had no pleats,
She let me hang Dad's handkerchiefs
And help her with the sheets.
She showed me how to shake each piece
And taught me how to place
Them corner over corner so
We'd save on pins and space.

And once the lines were full, we'd prop
Them up and lift them high
To keep the clothes from touching ground
While they were getting dry,
But checking often, taking down
Dry pieces, one by one,
To make room for the darker clothes
As Mom would get them done.
Then she would hang the blue jeans while
I matched up sock for sock;
And I'm still sure Mom had the neatest
Clotheslines on the block.

Now, when I need a break from all
Life's unrewarding chores,
I only have to take a basketful
Of clothes outdoors;
And though my coated lines don't rust,
I wipe them free of dew,
Place corner over corner just
The way Mom taught me to,

And let each pin do twice the work
While wishing Mom were there
To share the fresh-wet dampness mingled
With the morning air.

Good photographs depend not only on the quality of the film and proper use of the camera, but also on the skill of the photographer to watch for great shots and then have the spontaneity to click the shutter without hesitation. Likewise, good word pictures depend not only on the spontaneity of the writer, but also on proper use of the mind's camera, through observation and the gathering of images. The difference is that a moment in time missed by the photographer can never be recaptured. No matter what pains he goes to, to reenact the moment, if he fails to get the picture the first time, that moment is lost forever. Not so with the writer whose words can record moments in time, anytime.

On our most recent trip to Australia, for the Sydney 2000 Olympics, my husband and I bought an older model car and traveled up the coast, from Melbourne to Cairns. Along the way, my camera was poised, ready to not miss a single precious moment in time. But I *did* miss several: a farm woman returning from a sugarcane field with a turned-up apron full of short pieces of cane; a half-grown lamb, down on one knee, nudging milk from its mother's udder; a three-foot long goanna doubling back into the bush on a mountain road; a seagull halting in midair to scratch its belly; and the list goes on. Since it was impossible to recapture the moments on film, all I could do was capture the images with my mind's camera and record them as word pictures in my diary, under "Pictures I Missed." Most of those pictures are now being developed for a travelogue in poetry.

Think of your mind as a camera with a memory-sensitive, hair-trigger shutter. It is continually snapping pictures, capturing memories, good or bad, and storing them like microscopic images on film. But the beauty part of *this* camera is that it comes equipped not only with sophisticated video and audio capabilities, but also with the ability to record touch, taste, and smell, all of which can be described with *words*.

That's not to say that all of our cameras see and record things the same way. Just as photographers see things differently — some capturing only the main subject, others taking in the entire background or foreground — writers do the same. Give three different writers the same subject on which to elaborate and, chances are, you'll get three entirely different word pictures.

❖ Getting the Picture

Find an old family *snap*shot, preferably one of an ancestor whose face (or story) has always intrigued you, or consider checking the shelves of an antique store for a photo or tintype of someone else's ancestor. If possible, choose one that also has an interesting background. Let the images that form in your mind's camera develop into one or more word pictures, true or imagined, describing the ancestor *and* the background as you believe it related to that ancestor, getting as detailed as you care or dare to. Then use the word picture(s) to write a poem or an essay.

Chapter 5

Preparing the Darkroom

Your mission as writer or poet memoirist, should you wish to accept it, is to process, or develop, your stored images into word pictures and put them in a scrapbook, for others — especially your descendants — to read and enjoy. This scrapbook will be one, not of tangible items and souvenirs, but of written accounts developed from the stockpile of memories in your mind — that "darkroom" where images begin to take shape and cry to be let out.

Of course, most of your memory images, still in "negative" form, have probably been collecting dust or are buried beneath the debris of more recent thoughts and memories. All the more reason to start pulling them out, brushing them off, and getting them ready for processing.

You may have already begun to process some of your images into word pictures, by keeping a journal of some sort. If not, you may want to consider starting one right now. Begin by recording any memorable events in your life, good or bad. Dates don't matter, details do. But details don't always come easy, so just relax and write whatever you remember. The rest will come to you later.

My first attempts at poetry were mostly fantasies, for children, because I didn't think my memory was good enough to come up with poems about my past. At the same time, though, I started keeping a journal about my childhood, one that would allow me to index its entries so that I could find whatever I wanted, whenever I needed it. That's when I started to realize that the more I wrote, the more I remembered. Of course, after years of storing them away, the details I remember as being perfect probably aren't; but they are close enough to let me write stories and poems that hold the attention of my readers which, in a sense, is my secondary goal — second to recording them for my own satisfaction, for the privilege of passing them down to my descendants.

A simple word processing program made the job easier, allowing me to set up a journal by subjects rather than dates, e.g. Home, Mom, Dad, Descriptions of People, etc. Then I went back through the daily journal I had already been keeping and copied every smidgen of an entry that pertained to my childhood (all, of course, in the form of flashbacks, since I did not keep a journal as a youngster), setting aside everything else for future endeavors. With subjects as headings on the pages, and dates/near dates as subheadings, it was easy to go back and forth from written journal to word processor, adding bits and pieces of information to subjects as I found, or remembered, additional details.

Once you've learned how to let images form in your mind's camera, and once you've learned to develop those images into word pictures, the next step is to decide what types of pictures you want to put in your scrapbook: those depicting your childhood? your working life? your married life? travel adventures? or a combination of one or more?

Whatever genre or form you use—poems, anecdotes, essays, or stories—make your memories come alive by choosing your words well. Whether you intend merely to pass them on to your descendants, or to have them published for the world to read, rewrite and revise them until they sound like something *you'd* like to read, had they been written by someone else.

As you read over what you think is your final draft, don't be surprised if additional images keep popping up, wanting to be developed. While it doesn't *always* happen, it *will* happen when you least expect it.

Once your writings (in whatever form) begin to take shape, you may want to set them aside in yet another binder or file to which you can add a working title. The working title can be changed at any time and will give you the incentive to keep writing and keep adding your memories to it.

You may also want to arrange your memories in a logical, though not necessarily "chrono" logical, order and start an index. With hundreds of poems in my repertoire (not all to be included in my scrapbook, of course), I have chosen to use a spreadsheet to index them, mainly because I can sort the poems by title, subject, or category—a great asset when I have to search for a particular poem to read or print out, for a particular purpose.

While handheld cell devices are be-coming the norm for recording anything and everything, keep in mind that those devices can get lost or destroyed, taking your files with them. This book is written from the viewpoint of one who still prefers to hear the shuffling of papers and to see and feel inspiration flowing from the pen.

❖ Getting the Picture

Gather together *anything* you have previously written about your life—past, present, or future—and decide what type of scrapbook (or memoir) you want to end up with. If you have no set pattern or genre in mind, begin by shaping your word pictures into any form you feel comfortable with at the moment. For now, don't worry about how vague the details are, or how they sound. Just get the words on paper. Then, as more details come to mind, go back and add them to your notes.

Part II

Finding the Focus

Chapter 1

Unlocking the Past

Going Back Home

We can't go back home, they say. And, in many ways, that's true. But that old adage doesn't apply to writers who can put their thoughts and hearts on paper.

I have to admit that, since the day my mother sold our family home (though not until some fifteen years after my father died, and long after my sisters and I were all married), there is no way I can bring myself to go back there, physically. Not that my legs won't take me there, but even driving anywhere near the house makes me cringe because of what the new owners have not done in the way of preserving it. Its front porch pillars are rotting away at the base; its paint is peeling; and its roof is deteriorating. To add to the heartache, the huge white mulberry tree that my sisters and

I played in, under, and around was partially destroyed by wind and totally removed by the new owners. An oversized doghouse sits in its place.

The house was built by my grandfather, a local carpenter who built many of the houses in our hometown. But he had built *this* house especially for his own family, just before my father was born. In fact, my father was born there shortly after the house was finished.

When my grandparents died, the house was purchased by my aunt and uncle, who left the interior as it was, structurally, but who slathered every lateral foot of its otherwise perfect woodwork with the dark green paint of the era. When my parents bought the house, they remodeled it extensively, turning what was once a back porch into a modern kitchen with a tin roof (my favorite room, especially when it was raining); re-plastering and painting the walls; and removing every speck of depressing green paint from the woodwork — the reason my mother always claimed she hated any shade of green.

While I can't bring myself to step back into the yard physically, I *can* go back to it with my mind's camera, to record some of my favorite images.

Cinder Rocks and Hollyhocks

The yard where I grew up, it seems,
Held more than childhood hopes and dreams.
It didn't mean much to me then,
But, oh, to be back there again:
The orchard, green with apple trees;
Fresh rhubarb and white mulberries;
The cistern with its iron lid;
Sweet lilacs where the kittens hid.

The alley near the garbage pit
Seemed then of little benefit,
Except where spikes of hollyhocks
Emerged from sand and cinder rocks;
For Mother taught us how to take
Their blossoms and their buds to make
The daintiest of crimson dolls
With fine-spun gowns and parasols.
Beneath the mulberry's drooping limb,
We'd fill Mom's washtub to the brim
And, with the water still aswirl,
Set every lacey doll awhirl.
On that transparent ballroom floor,
Kid fantasies took wing to soar
Above the lowly hollyhocks
That grew up through the cinder rocks.

Likewise, I *can* go back to our family home through my writings, walking through every foot of its homey interior, using my mind's camera to re-record every detail that I can recall about it. I need only step up, open the door, and turn on the lights.

Turning on the Lights

Shock and *disappointment* can't begin to describe how I felt when I realized, some twenty years ago, that I have very few "telling" photographs of the home where my two older sisters and I grew up. I have one of the outside of our house, taken with my Kodak Brownie camera, and I have miscellaneous indoor pictures of special occasions, like birthdays and anniversaries. But I don't have the deep-down pictures of what home was all about: the kitchen where all five of us sat around the table, in the exact same chairs, to eat at the exact same time every morning and evening; where springtime sprinkles sounded like pounding rain on the tin roof of what had once been a porch; and where family meetings took place when there was a problem, or important planning to be done. Or of the living room, with its AM-only tube radio set where, every evening after supper, we'd climb aboard the floral design of our magic '42 vintage carpet, to ride along with *The Lone Ranger* or shudder in the darkness of *The Shadow* and *Inner Sanctum*, until we'd fall asleep and have to be roused or carried to our beds.

Those were the common events of our everyday lives, events that none of us ever thought of recording on film. So, for fear of losing them altogether, I resorted to writing word pictures — detailed descriptions of *everything* I could remember about *anything*. And, by further developing those word pictures into poems, I have, in a sense, been able to preserve portions of my childhood that might otherwise be lost.

If I Could Go Back in Time

I don't believe in "time machines"
In picture shows and such;
Most things that reek "impossible"
I never think of much.

Yet if I had a time machine,
I know just where I'd go:
Directly to the house where I
Was brought up years ago.

I'd go back to the kitchen where
Our old tin roof would sound
Like someone beating on a pan
When rain began to pound;

Where Mom would have the table set,
And supper right at four;
And we'd all gather there the moment
Dad walked through the door.

I'd go back to the days when,
After supper, we'd all go
Into the "middle room" where we'd
Turn on the radio.
We kids, in our pajamas,

Would soon sprawl out on the floor
To hear *The Shadow* and the
Inner Sanctum's "squeaking door";

Lone Ranger and his sidekick
Making yet another leap—
With *"Hi-Yo, Silver!"* on our lips,
We'd drift right off to sleep.

Before I knew it, I'd be safely
Cradled in Dad's arms
And carried to my bed, where
Flannel sheets would keep me warm.

I don't believe in time machines,
But if I'd ever find
That one could take me home again,
I really wouldn't mind.

My desire and, more accurately, my *need* to re-create those pictures, was hampered only by my own inner argument that some memories surely lie too deep to be recovered. It was one thing, I found, as I sat with readied pen and blank paper, to recall highlights of special events. But it would be quite another to dig up the minute details of everyday events that make printed pictures what they actually are—short stories of the past. Yet, once I really started searching, I found memories hiding everywhere. I only had to hunt them down, drag them out, and brush them off. My hopes are that this book will encourage and prepare you for doing the same.

❖ Getting the Picture
Go back, mentally, if not physically, to the home where you were brought up and "walk" through it, room by room. Let the images that form in your mind's camera develop into one or more word pictures describing the house as you remember it. Then use the word picture(s) to write a poem or an essay.

Chapter 2

Digging Up the Bones

Hunting for Buried Treasure

It is no secret that, until recently, even with organized garbage dumps, and garbage trucks that made pickups on a regular basis, many people in rural areas still dug pits and buried their trash in their own back yards. Out of sight, out of mind; but not always, and not forever, for small, heavy objects have a tendency to work their way to the surface.

Years ago, we kept our young son occupied by giving him a quarter for every coffee can full of glass he picked up in our unpaved, well-packed, sand driveway. But no matter how much he picked up, more fragments appeared. Especially during hard rains, scraps of history — from everyone who ever lived on this hill — get pounded to the surface. It isn't unusual to find square nails, as well as recognizable shards of pottery, porcelain figurines, and children's toys. In fact, when we used a trencher to run a new water line, its tines brought up enough bits and pieces of the hill's past to send us running for shovels and digging a wider trench.

In a cross section of one dumpsite, we found clear glass medicine bottles; brown Iodine and Clorox bottles, unscathed except for their missing corks; a 2 oz. LISTERINE bottle with raised lettering and Bakelite lid still intact; opaque cold cream jars; lids of old jars and jars with no lids; percolator parts and pieces of china; slow-rotting tires and decaying inner tubes; and nail polish and food coloring bottles.

Further endeavors with a metal detector turned up a chipped, blue granite dipper. And yet another excavation turned up a large foundation stone from a farmhouse that burned on the very spot where our house sits today. Every fragment of a *scrap* gives us a little more insight into the history of this hill and the people who lived here before us—of approximate times; of ages and physical conditions; of events that took place. But they are only indications of what *real* treasures might still be hidden beneath the ground we tread every day.

Within the mind's cameras are bits and pieces of the past, images still in negative form, which are continually shuffled around or buried by newer, more recent recordings of thought and memory. When agitated or disturbed, some rise slowly to the surface, like heavy objects during a rain. Others have to be mined by digging and prying. Either way, memories are nothing less than bits of gold waiting to be mined from the veins of life.

As I started jotting down notes about my relationship with my mother—like how she always found time for me, no matter how busy she was—I was overwhelmed with flashbacks of how she used to braid my hair, or roll it up in rags, to make long curls; of how she tied the bows on the backs of my cotton dresses when I was getting ready for school; and of how she took the time to cut miniature bandages from white adhesive tape when the soft rubber fingers, elbows, and heels of the doll I called Mikey began to deteriorate and let the stuffing spew out.

Mikey is the *Effanbee* doll I found under the tree on my fifth Christmas. I still can't part with him, even though his composition face has shattered into a zillion hairline cracks, and his marble-blue eyes cross at the slightest bump or jar. He now sits on an antique chest of drawers, still sporting the adhesive tape bandages *and* the coal black hairpiece that Mom cut from fake fur and glued over his painted-on, shattered hair. So it was easy to come up with a word picture that perfectly described my mother, and a poem which has since found its way into table magazines, books, newspapers, church bulletins, and family history books.

Mother's Hands

Mother's hands were busy hands,
But never did they fail
To take the time to tie a bow
Or braid a loose pigtail.

And never did those hands refuse
To soothe a fevered brow,
So even injured dolls pulled through
In Mother's hands, somehow.
Dear Lord, I pray, as years go by,
Whatever life's demands,
That I may give just half the love
I've found in Mother's hands.

❖ Getting the Picture

Browse through an antique store, searching for an item that reminds you of your own past: a toy you played with as a child, a tool you worked with at some time in your life, or something you remember your parents or grandparents using. From the images that form in your mind's camera, develop one or more word pictures describing the item and how it affected your life. Then use the word picture(s) to write a poem or an essay.

Spading Up the Garden

Dad always planted a vegetable garden, sometimes a fairly big one that took up nearly a fourth of our quarter block. While he and Mom hoed and raked and gathered the harvest, my middle sister and I busied ourselves with our dolls, or with taking our dime store turtle for an outing in Mom's flowerbed. But the year we decided to plant some flowers of our own, Dad reserved two rows in his garden, just for us. (That our oldest sister was already a teenager by this time accounts for the fact that she does not appear in many of my childhood poems.)

Our middle sister has always had a green thumb, and I still depend on her advice when it comes to flowers. However, that year, I decided that the zinnias she chose to plant were a little too ordinary, so I chose to plant snapdragons instead. The trouble was, my seeds failed to germinate, maybe because I planted them too deeply or didn't water them enough. At any rate, years later, when I started "getting the picture," I was more than prepared to write a poem about the entire planting and weeding episode.

From Seedlings to "Wheedlings"

My sister and I went through many a stage
Where it seemed that we differed in little but age
For, in most things, we two stuck together like glue
Yet, like most healthy sisters, we fought to outdo
One another in games we created for fun—
Though, in all but my daydreams, I lost every one.

I remember one spring, when Dad's garden was in,
She came up with a game I just knew I could win:
We would each plant the seeds of the flower we liked best,
Then we'd put our young gardening skills to the test.
In a matter of days, we'd be able to see
Just whose thumb was the greenest. How hard could it be?

So Dad bought us the packets of seeds that we chose,
And we planted them all in two, neat little rows;
But my knowledge of flowers could never suffice,
So I had to depend on my sister's advice.
Hand in hand, every morning, we checked on those seeds.
Then one day she discovered some troublesome 'weeds'
That she said would take over the space in my row
If I left them there and, to this day, I don't know
If the tiny green leaves that had started to sprout
Were snapdragons or weeds, but she helped pull them out.
Then I waited for days while her zinnias grew tall
And the row that I'd planted grew nothing at all.

Now if stories have morals, then this one might read:
"Never ask your opponent to help you succeed."
But, then, who would have guessed that a weed-pulling scene
Would be foremost in coaxing *my* thumb to turn green
So that, years down the line, I'd be picking bouquets
From the gardens of memories I learned how to raise.

❖ Getting the Picture

Walk through a flower garden or a greenhouse and browse around, observing the smells, colors, and textures of the flowers. Choose one flower and examine it closely. Let the images that form in your mind's camera develop into one or more word pictures describing the intricate petals and their leaves. Include any insect activity—honeybees, ladybugs, butter-flies, etc.—that might be taking place in, or around, the flowers. Then use the word picture(s) to write a poem or an essay.

Reading Old Letters

As Mother's Days, Christmases, and birthdays came around, I dug deeper and deeper into my storehouse of memories to write poems for my mother, who took great pride in the fact that I remembered so much of what she and Dad had done for us as children. We had never been rich, but neither were we poor, so although we didn't have everything we wanted, we had most everything we needed. What I began to realize, though, was that neither of our parents ever had to *make an effort* to do things for us. They just did them.

Mom made most of our clothes, as well as our dolls' clothes, and every apron I ever saw my grandma wear. I never thought much about the doll clothes until the day I unpacked my Toni doll, which had been stored away for some thirty years. In the box beside her were the original plastic curlers and end tissues, plus a nearly-full bottle of Toni Permanent solution, for making lasting curls in her long, blonde hair. But the doll and her accessories were not what made me cry. It was the clothes.

Our son had just opened his own chiropractic office. It had been a struggle for us, financially, to help him through medical school, but we willingly, and thankfully, did whatever it took. Now, as I held the varied wardrobe of handmade doll clothes in my hands, it dawned on me just how many willing sacrifices of time, money, and sanity my mother must have made for my sisters and me while we were growing up. Yet I had never really thanked her for any of it. That day, as I hand-washed and ironed those doll clothes, I stopped often to jot down images that formed in my mind's camera.

Letter Overdue, Postmarked 1992

Mom, I ironed my doll clothes today;
It's been years since I put them away,
But they're still just as dear
As my memories are clear,
For it seems it was just yesterday.

As I unpacked the box where they'd been,
I recounted my childhood again;

But when "handmade, not bought"
Entered into my thought,
Overwhelming nostalgia set in;
For I knew I could never replace
What you'd made from old dresses, and lace;
There were hats, coats and shirts,
Jackets, dresses and skirts,
With their buttons and snaps still in place.

After years of doll use, they were worn,
But looked great for the treatment they'd borne;
Moths had taken their toll
On the ones made of wool,
And one red and white sun dress was torn.
But I washed them all out, just for fun,
And had started to press the first one
When tears, blurring my sight,
Shed a different light
On how much, as a mother, you'd done.

It was never unusual for you
To do housework and make doll clothes, too,
But you painted and baked,
Washed the windows and raked,
Besides all that friends asked you to do.
Why you never got cross or upset
Is an unexplained mystery yet,
For you seemed not to mind
The monotonous grind
Of what most mothers tend to regret.

For an instant, I saw you back there,
Where I watched from my perch on the stair,

Showing me how to press
Tiny sleeves on the dress
That you'd made for my best doll to wear;
And then letting me finish the rest,
Keeping check as I ironed my best,
While you placed on the shelf
What you'd ironed yourself
And I put what I'd learned to the test.

Mom, I ironed my doll clothes today.
It's been years since I packed them away,
But they're still just as dear
As my memories are clear,
For it seems it was just yesterday.

❖ Getting the Picture

Try to recall something that your parents (or someone else) did for you that was not required but that they did merely because they wanted to. Let the images that form in your mind's camera develop into one or more word pictures. Then use the word picture(s) to write a poem or an essay.

Chapter 3

Poking Around the Cellar

Savoring Memories

Back when air conditioning was reserved for movie theaters and exclusive hotels, my family spent the better part of the sweltering days of July and August in our basement. Down there, cement block walls and the concrete floor absorbed below-ground temperatures, rather than the relentless rays of the sun. Those were the canning months anyway and, near the end of the day, Mom would convert her canning table into a supper table. At the same time, she'd cook our supper on the three-burner, cast iron gas stove that Dad had bolted onto a square gray cabinet he'd built especially for it. Beneath the stove, gray doors hid oversized pots and pans reserved for canning.

From the time canning season started, until Mom had put up her end-of-the-garden salad, the lingering smells of tomatoes, green beans, cherries, apples, grapes, peaches, and cucumbers in brine (or pickling spices), permeated the air and the bare rafters.

The lure of the canning kettle, the frequent stirring and skimming, and the smell of the pink-tinted steam rising from simmering tomatoes or juice, kept me near Mom's side during morning canning sessions, especially in early September, after my sisters were in school. While Mom was sorting, coring, and quartering tomatoes, she let me fill her laundry tubs with hot, sudsy water and submerge our chosen mix of jars, for washing. My favorites were the squatty, round Hills Brothers and Folgers Coffee jars, with narrow mouths that I could get my hand down inside, to clean, and that held a smidgen more than a quart of juice. Then there were the taller peanut butter jars, with "quilted," raised diamond patterns on all four sides. And always, once the filled jars were set aside to cool and seal, there would be a cup or so of warm, salted-just-right juice that Mom couldn't squeeze into the last jar no matter how she tried, and that she would pour into her "tin" (actually, aluminum) measuring cup, for us to share.

Sipping Memories

Dear Mom, Today I'm right back home again.
It's summer, and I'm only nine or ten,
"Down th' basement," where I'll spend the day with you,
Learning eagerly a canning skill or two:

There are coffee jars we've transferred from the shelf
To the rinse tubs, where I'll wash them by myself
As you're filling kettles, where you cut and core
Two bushels of tomatoes (maybe more),
While hints of pickling spices best reveal
What's recently been packed and under seal.

My thoughts are stirred by tiny pits and scars
In the metal cup you dipped to fill those jars -
And steam that scents my kitchen as I skim
Tomato juice now frothing at the brim.
Still, it isn't jars or cups or scents, I find,
That bring the dearest memories to mind,
But the steaming juice you'd leave inside the cup
For us to share, once the last jar was filled up,
So we could taste the canning of the day
Before we put the kettles all away.

Now I'd surely linger longer if I could,
For the smells of going home are always good;
But the metal cup is ready to be dipped,
And more memories are waiting to be sipped.

I don't remember which came first — the poem, or my determination to relive one of those tomato-juice-canning days in my own kitchen.

I only know that before I started washing, sorting, and quartering tomatoes that day, I made sure there were three treasured *scraps* close at hand: one of the twelve squatty coffee jars Mom had passed on to me, along with her last box of BERNARDIN No. 63 Snap Lids — the only ones, very small and no longer available — that fit those jars, *and* Mom's tin measuring cup.

Despite warnings not to, I still open-kettle can my tomatoes and juice. So, as the juice simmered on this day, I paid particular attention to the familiar aroma rising from my dishpan-type canning pans. And once the juice was skimmed, and several wide mouth jars were filled, it was time to fill and seal the coffee jar. But most important of all was the cup or so of juice that I deliberately set aside, in Mom's measuring cup, to be slowly sipped once my canning pans were all washed up. That coffee jarful of tomato juice, along with the measuring cup, is pictured in the framed copy of "Sipping Memories," which now hangs over my writing desk.

By the end of every September, Mom had created a sparkling glass rainbow of peaches and green beans, tomatoes, pickles, and jellies — all hidden behind the wainscot doors of the storage cabinet beneath our basement stairs. But the glass rainbow was not all that survived behind those gray doors. Water bugs hung out there, too, in the cool darkness. So, whenever I opened those doors to retrieve a jar of anything for Mom, I always gave the bugs time to retreat into the more distant darkness before I reached inside.

Then, too, there were the dumber bugs that ended up inside jars that had been emptied, washed, and returned to storage. It was a mystery to me how they could crawl up the outside of the glass jar to get in, yet they couldn't crawl up the inside to get back out. At any rate, their lifeless black shells were always there, waiting, sometimes laced in with spider webs, when we retrieved the jars for the next summer's canning. I have since learned to keep my empty canning jars clean by putting the washed lids back on them until they are ready to be washed and filled again.

❖ Getting the Picture

If possible, take out a jar of home-canned fruit, vegetables, or jelly that you or someone else preserved. Place it on the table in front of you. Study it well as you mentally go through the steps that it took, from harvest to canning, to end up with that single jar. Let the images that form in your mind's camera develop into one or more word pictures describing the person who did the work of preserving, plus your anticipation of opening the jar and tasting the food inside. Then use the word picture(s) to write a poem or an essay.

Opening Doors

To the right of the wainscot-door cabinets, and halfway up the cement block wall, was a smaller, single wainscot door that led to a crawl space beneath our kitchen. That closed-in space, with its dirt floor and deep earthen smell, had no windows, vents, or electric lights. It had become the depositing place for two items that had belonged to my paternal grandparents, and that no one, including my parents, had any use for but didn't want to throw away either, namely, a white-enameled chamber pot and a wooden steamer trunk slathered with gray paint.

Both remained in the crawl space until several years after my father died. Only then did I see the uppermost contents of the trunk: a weighty knee-length coat that my grandmother had made for herself, plus her hat and some handmade dresses, all of which were given to my niece and ultimately disposed of by my sister. I became the recipient of the trunk itself, although I must admit that, at the time, I had little use for the rest of its contents and removed them all to storage so that I could refinish the trunk.

Not until I started researching my family history did I realize that the steamer trunk had, doubtless, been hauled to this country from Switzerland or England, by one or the other of my paternal *great*-grandparents. *Then* it was time to pull from storage the items for which I'd formerly had little use.

There was a well-worn pair of my grandmother's black lace-up shoes; a black, silkish scarf, the likes of which I have never seen before or since (bearing large red leaves and small white snowflakes from the center to one tapered end and small red leaves and large white snowflakes from the center to the other tapered end); two bonnets — a plain white one, for nightwear, and a blue and white checkered one with a Red Cross pin still attached; a green, celluloid-covered jewelry box with hinged lid and hidden base compartment; three handmade bead necklaces; and, best of all, a pair of black leather boys' shoes, undoubtedly my father's Sunday best, with scuffed toes, and smudges of clay still clinging to their soles.

As I studied those shoes, from heels to toes, the images that formed in my mind's camera were endless. I could see my dad (probably) attending church with his parents and then going to his grandmother's house for Sunday dinner; (possibly) playing marbles with his older brother, or with cousins, who would also have been there; and his mother putting the leather shoes away for the last time, with bits of clay still clinging to their soles, when he had outgrown them. While I couldn't bring myself to write what I didn't really know for sure, I could write what I *did* know.

Dad's Sunday Shoes

In one corner of my bedroom, there's
A trunk that holds a pair
Of little boys' black leather shoes
My father used to wear.
Their soles still hold a tiny bit
Of 1920s clay
That was there the day my grandma put
Those Sunday shoes away.
For years the shoes lay hidden
Neath the clothes, where they'd been placed—
Until the day I found them with
Their strings still neatly laced
And knew the scuffs and scratches that
Had not been polished out
Were telltale evidence of what
Dad's boyhood was about.

In thought, I reassure myself
That Grandma must have known
Her son would have much bigger shoes
To fill once he was grown;
Yet, in my fondest daydreams, I
Still wish that *she* could see
How he grew to be the kind of friend
That every dad should be.

Although the items in the trunk gave me a glimpse of my dad's childhood, and of my grand*mother,* they said nothing of my grand-*father*. But the commercial fishing nets and hand-carved duck decoys that hung from the rafters of our basement, along with images and descriptions relayed by those who knew him, did. Those images are depicted in the poem "Grandpa Simon," in a previous chapter.

At the opposite end of our basement, under the front porch, there was a second crawl space. Although this one had a full-sized door about two feet off the floor, the "crawl space" itself was only deep enough to half-stand once you were inside. The only step up to the door was a coffin-like toolbox that held my grandfather's carpenter tools: wood planes, hand drills, and rasps he most likely used when he was building houses. That toolbox is still intact, waiting to provide my mind's camera with untold images.

❖ Getting the Picture
Is there a door from your past that holds a certain mystery? Perhaps it was the door to your grandmother's attic, which seemed overwhelmingly large to you as a child, or the tiny door of a jewelry box that you weren't allowed to touch? Let the images that form in your mind's camera develop into one or more word pictures describing that or any other

mysterious door; what you finally found (or imagined) was behind it; and how its mystery affected you. Then use the word picture(s) to write a poem or an essay.

Sweeping the Corners

Besides the smells of *Dreft* Laundry Detergent, the *Sweetheart* Soap with which Mom bathed us in the laundry tubs once the laundry was done, and fresh-wet clothes strung out on lines in our basement, there was yet another smell, of coal dust. The coal bin, which was a small, unheated room near the furnace, was the only area of the basement that was closed off. Its flat-white, coal-smudged door was usually kept closed, especially on winter days when coal had just been, or was about to be, delivered. On the outside wall of the coal bin, a square black iron door, hinged at the bottom and protruding slightly to the outside, could be laid open to form a chute.

Coal fed through the chute quickly covered the floor of the bin and ran black into its corners, pressing against the inside of the smudgy-white door, so that the first time the door was opened a river of the black stuff fanned out onto the basement floor like a small delta. Dad always scooped up the delta and shoveled it back into the bin, or directly into the furnace, so that the door could be closed again. But coal wasn't all that got tossed into the flames *or* into my mind's camera when I took an imaginary walk back through that basement.

Burned Up

We often put Dad at a loss
To try to get his point across,
Though once he thought he'd found a cure
For making absolutely sure
That he was fully understood —
He cut a paddle out of wood
And hung it in the entranceway
Where we could see it every day.

Now it was Mom who made the fuss,
For we were sure that none of us
Would ever have the privilege
Of meeting with that paddle's edge.
But all too soon, to my distress,
My natural, quiet stubbornness
Was slightly more than Dad could stand
And things, it seemed, got out of hand.

'Twas I who felt that paddle's sting!
Then Mom stepped in and grabbed the thing!
She opened up the furnace door
And tossed that paddle in before
Dad ever had a chance to say
A word about it! Anyway,

Mom's point was made—quite well, at that,
But Dad's was, too, from where I sat.

On summer days, while Mom was canning, or on winter evenings when she and Dad worked side by side at his workbench—he, building cabinets for our newly remodeled kitchen; she, whittling pairs of wild ducks from blocks of wood—we played on the other side of the basement, in a corner that had become our playhouse. Our cement-gray walls held everything from dolls to furniture: the table and chairs Dad had made; a small wicker rocker Mom had upholstered with heavy maroon tapestry, to match the doll-sized couch she had made from scratch; and the oversized tricycle that was just the right size for circling the furnace. But on summer days, when Mom was busy somewhere other than the basement, we'd get the urge to play outdoors, though not without every last toy from that basement corner.

Loads and Loads of Fun

Back when kids could create
Their own fun, we would wait
For a day when we both felt inclined
To play house out of doors,
With trees shading our floors
And the cats to play host while we dined.

We'd start early enough
To transfer all our stuff,
Although time was the least of our cares,
With the door to be juggled
While both of us struggled
To drag all we owned up the stairs
And then lug it outside
To the landing with pride,
Where invisible walls would expand
To hold all that we thought
Should be wrestled and brought
To the make-believe house we had planned.

Besides one rocking chair
And a sofa to bear,
There were dolls with their bottles and clothes,
And the dishes we'd squeeze
In for afternoon teas—
To take place anytime that we chose;
Plus the things Dad had done
That made playing more fun—
Like the table and chairs built for two;

In a much lighter load
Came rag dolls Mom had sewed
From the curls on their heads to their shoes;
And our trike, last of all,
That we both had to haul,
Just in case we had "errands" to run,
Though, by then, all our shade
Was beginning to fade
In the heat of the late morning sun;

So we'd leave all to go
Back inside, even though
There were loads of fun left in the day,
For we'd find, by the time
We had made that last climb,
We were simply...too...tired...to...play...

❖ Getting the Picture
Go to a basement or cellar, with a flashlight, if necessary, and search for at least one object that sparks a memory of your past. Let the images that form in your mind's camera develop into one or more word pictures describing the object, how it was used by you or someone else, and what affect it had/has on your life, past or present. Then use the word picture(s) to write a poem or an essay.

Opening the Cistern

In one small, dark corner of our basement, between the wainscot doors that held back the dreaded water bugs, and the high wainscot door that led to the crawl space under the kitchen, there was an inconspicuous pitcher pump. With a little priming, the pump would draw extremely cold, soft rainwater, which we used for washing our hair, from the cistern in the back yard.

    In the back yard, the only evidence of the cistern was a round, rolled cement edging that stood no taller than the grass. It had a diamond plate steel lid that never shifted once it was in place. The only time we ever got a glimpse of the cistern's inside—that deep well lined with red brick—was when Dad slid the lid away, to check the water level and make sure that the downspouts from the house were draining into it properly. Although he had no fears of the cistern caving in, he was always careful not to drive over it. Not so with some of our delivery people, however.

In the late '40s and early '50s, delivery trucks were a common sight in our neighborhood—especially those of the milkman, who delivered quart bottles topped with rich cream, and the bread man, who delivered all types of baked goods, including torpedo-shaped donuts called Filled Fish.

When television commercials introduced Omar bread to the Midwest, with a whistle and a, "*Hey, Mom, here comes the Omar Man!*" **(sss)**, the bread man's title was quickly upgraded to "the Omar man." And, while I can't speak for anyone else's Omar man, ours took the company slogan so seriously that, at least once, he literally drove his panel truck right up into our yard and stopped *right on top* of our cistern.

The Omar Man

The milkman rarely
came to the door but merely
left Mom's standard order of
cream-topped milk
on our front porch
and went on.

The bread man,
on the other hand,
always knocked on the back door,
to see if she needed extra bread,
or rolls, or maybe even
a package of Filled Fish
for kids who loved their
fluffy white filling.
But when Omar Bread
was on the rise and
painting our town with
its new slogan,
Mom had a shock in store
when the bread man's knock
gave way to the *thump!*
of his truck
jumping the curb,
and his sing-song blurb:
"From the oven to your door!"

> *(sss)* I was less than satisfied with my first and subsequent renditions of "The Omar Man." Even my word pictures, which described his shocking but unforgettable actions, were missing something. Only after the poem seemed to start coming together did the old TV commercial trickle back into my mind's camera, bringing with it the image of a young boy and the sound of a whistle followed by, *"Hey, Mom, here comes the Omar Man!"*

Besides food deliveries, there were door-to-door salesmen, like the *Watkins* man and the *Fuller Brush* man who, once they got a foot in the door, managed to get a suitcase full of goods in, too. Year after year, other door-to-doors kept cropping up, with new ideas and new products. One of the last salesmen who came to our house showed up when Mom was on her hands and knees, painting our front porch. While she insisted that she didn't have time to stop and talk to him, he insisted that she should take time. He turned tail immediately when she threatened to paint his trousers. But other salesmen came with products no mother could resist — products whose images still make their way into my mind's camera.

One of a Kind

In the days of Fuller Brush,
when salesmen went
door to door
to pitch their wares,
they found our house an easy mark,
for even Dad would let them in and
listen to their spiels.

But it was through the
fly-by-night ones who came by day
that Mom got caught off guard
and ordered such things as
the framed oval picture of
my sister at age two,
that hung on our wall for as long
as I could remember.

It was easy to see then, how,
years later, she got taken in
with the idea of a doll that would look
exactly like any one of her children;
and why she ran to retrieve
a picture from the family album;
and why she ordered and paid for
the doll, right then and there.
It arrived by mail and was by far
the ugliest doll I never played with.
Her face was mine, but only in the form
of the black and white photo, now tinted pink
and pressed flatly to her head
behind a stiff plastic shield
whose edges were hidden
by bonnet and bow.

On that day, it appeared
that the joke was on us;
yet today, she sits among
other dolls her age,
looking smug in the knowledge that
she's one of a kind
in two different worlds—
hers, and mine.

❖ Getting the Picture

Think back, about an item that was delivered to your home when you were a youngster. Let the images that form in your mind's camera develop into one or more word pictures describing the person who delivered it and the reaction, happy or sad, of whoever it was for. Then use the word picture(s) to write a poem or an essay.

Ransacking the Closet

The old steamer trunk that was taken from the crawl space in our family home now sits in a corner of my bedroom. Among other things, it holds the last cobalt-blue bottle of *Evening in Paris* perfume, complete with 25¢ sticker, which Mom purchased at one of Pekin's dime stores. It takes me back to the vanity where she'd powder her nose and put on a touch of lipstick and a dab of *Evening in Paris* whenever we were going someplace special. Sometimes I'd sit on a corner of the bed and watch her. Other times

I'd brush my own long hair (100 strokes to make it shine, Mom always said), or rummage through her walk-in type closet to find a pair of open-toed, high-heeled shoes and go clunking around the bedroom while she was finishing up.

Filling Mother's Shoes

When I was just a little girl,
I'd dress in Mother's clothes
And try to look like Mother from
My head down to my toes.
I'd put on Mother's lipstick and
Tie ribbons in my hair,
And try to fill the high-heeled shoes
That Mother let me wear.

Now playing house was twice the fun
In Mother's cotton lace
And, in my world of make-believe,
I walked with Mother's grace;
For though her shoes were much too big,
I felt the difference slight,
Yet hoped next time I'd put them on
They'd fit my feet just right.
I don't recall the day that I
Put Mother's shoes away
And realized that filling them
Was more than child's play.
But every now and then, when life
Gets difficult, I muse
On childhood things and grown-up dreams
Of filling Mother's shoes.

My own closets now allow for a fair amount of rummaging, with unlabeled boxes to be opened and checked periodically, in an effort to refresh my memory. But there are also familiar ones that hold my most prized Christmas orna-ments — those made by our son in elementary school. Those ornaments long ago sparked images of my own childhood Christmases.

A Penny for Our Thoughts

Mom taught us right from wrong, good manners,
And the alphabet;
Dad taught us how to net a fish,
And I'll not soon forget
The year that he decided it
Was time for us to know
That sharing is the caring part
Of Christmas time; and so,
To teach the gift of giving that
He wanted us to learn,
He gave us two half-dollars that
We didn't have to earn.
He said that we could buy a gift
To hide beneath the tree.
We'd mark it with a tag that read
"To Mom" from Shirl and me.

We tramped through snow to reach our favorite
Five and ten cent store,
Though neither of us had a clue
What we were looking for.

We searched each bin and cubbyhole,
Each counter and each shelf
To find a gift that Mom would never
Purchase for herself;
Passing over useful things, like
Crochet hooks and thread,
To buy a tube of lipstick that
Was *absolutely* red;

Then searching more, throughout the store,
Till we agreed to choose
A gadget that we hoped was something
Mom could surely use.
We couldn't tell just what it was
Or even what it fit
But bought it anyway because
We liked the looks of it.

The hardest part was waiting as
Mom opened what we'd bought,
While hoping Dad approved of what
We'd learned from what he'd taught.
And sure enough, Mom was surprised.
And so were Dad and Jean.
The lipstick was the brightest red
They said they'd ever seen.
Still, Mom consented graciously
To trying it, but when
The day was over, I don't think
We saw that red again.
As for the gadget, Mom was quite
Familiar with its use:
Its holes would let her sprinkle clothes,
To iron wrinkles loose.

For years I wondered how Mom kept
From laughing every time
She thought about those gifts we'd purchased
At the "five and dime."
But long before our son was old
Enough to shop alone,
He gave his dad a Christmas gift
He'd thought of on his own.
He'd wrapped it up and tied it with
A little piece of string,
And he could hardly wait to see
Fred open up the thing.
The marble and the penny tucked
Inside the plastic case
Took on the love that we still see
Reflected in his face;
Yet, to this day, he wonders why
That gift still sparks a tear
When I unpack and hang it on
Our Christmas tree each year.

❖ Getting the Picture

If you don't already have one, go to an antique store and find a Christmas ornament or decoration that reminds you of a childhood Christmas. From the images that form in your mind's camera, write one or more word pictures describing why that particular ornament caught your eye, the memory it brings back to you, and the effect that memory has on you now. Then use the word picture(s) to write a poem or an essay.

Climbing the Spiral Staircase

By the time my mother had to give up housekeeping, the corner of her house she had reserved for craft materials was overflowing with yet-to-be-used quilt pieces, bags of macramé cord and beads, and kiln-dried ceramic pieces waiting to be painted. In addition, the loft above her spiral staircase was cluttered with oil paints, finished and partially-finished canvasses, and antique frames. When I offered to do some deep-down sorting and cleaning of those areas, with the promise of throwing nothing away without her approval, she took me up on the deal. But I wasn't prepared for what I found, especially when I got to the two locked steamer trunks that had, for years, served as tables as well as storage boxes.

The trunks were filled to the brim with even more scraps of material she had saved for making quilt pieces. But these weren't *ordinary* scraps, like the ones in her craft corner. *These* were scraps she had saved since I was a little girl, scraps I recognized from dresses she had made for me and my sisters; from aprons she had made for Grandma, the last of which now hangs on a hook in my bedroom; from clothes she had made for my *Toni* doll; and from (*sss*) remnants of the drapes that hung in the dining room we never used as such and ended up calling "the middle room."

Box by box, and bag by bag, I carried the pieces downstairs, to where Mom was resting. While we talked, I sorted and ironed every single *scrap*, overwhelmed with images that flooded my mind's camera, and word pictures that I could hardly wait to get on paper.

> *(sss)* I was proofreading the previous paragraph, about dresses, aprons, and doll clothes, when I remembered a piece of floral-on-gray, tapestry-like material that I'd found inside one of Mom's steamer trunks. While I had vaguely recognized the pattern at the time, I had failed to ask Mom about it. As a result, I have never been able to put my finger on what that particular material was from—until *now*, when a new image flashed into my mind's camera: that of the *drapes* that hung in the middle room of our house. More proof that writing whatever you can remember brings back even more details to add to the story.

Aprons and Things

Dear Mom, Today I traveled back in time,
On memories that didn't cost a dime.
The roads I took were paved with bits and scraps
Of cotton prints that furnished flawless maps.

It started when I opened lids and locks
Of trunks where you had emptied box on box
Of sewing scraps you've never thrown away
Because they'll go to make a quilt someday.

I must admit, I simply couldn't see
How scraps of cloth could warrant lock and key,
Until my fingers smoothed the wrinkled shreds
Of pictures tucked away among their threads.

I saw myself, in pigtails, as I played
With dolls dressed up in clothes that you had made;
And, in their midst, the rag doll I still prize,
With curly hair and hand-embroidered eyes;

I caught a glimpse or two of Grandma there,
In aprons that you'd made for her to wear;
Then lingered through a printed potpourri
Of clothes you'd sewn for Jean and Shirl and me.

Each print still held the common thread of love
That all the things you ever made were of;
And it's that thread of love that always brings
Me back, full circle, to your apron strings.

Your apron strings were something of the kind
That let me be myself and trail behind,
And yet, when I preferred, they could be tied
To let me cling securely to your side.

There never was a thing I'd rather do
Than spend my childhood growing up like you,
And it's a cinch that love will always flow
Through our memories of fifty years ago.

When the poem was finished, I couldn't let go of the desire to make a quilt from the special scraps in the steamer trunks. The trouble was, I wasn't into quilting. I remembered being at a quilting bee with Mom when I was nine or ten years old. The aunt who had sewn the quilt pieces together had given me a threaded needle, and a thimble, and let me try my hand at making straight rows of tiny, even stitches. Good experience, but I wasn't ready to tackle a full-sized quilt on my own, especially when Mom couldn't help me with it. But there was no reason why she couldn't oversee the project. That's when I took it upon myself, under her supervision, to make three doll-sized quilts — one for each of my sisters, and one for me.

The fun came in laying out 2½-inch squares of colorful prints, in three totally different arrangements. The work came in hand-stitching those pieces together (no machine stitching allowed, by order of Mom). The tension came in the quilting itself, in making those straight lines of tiny, even stitches. The reward came in watching Mom stitch the last short diagonal line in the corner of each quilt. The joy came in our presenting the finished quilts to my sisters, along with copies of "Aprons and Things."

❖ Getting the Picture

Find an old quilt, preferably one made by an ancestor, and look at the stitches. Try to determine if the quilting was done by one pair of hands or by many. You'll be able to tell by the consistency (or not) of the stitches: all the same, one pair of hands; different sized stitches and/or spacing, two or more pairs of hands. Then try to imagine the many sewing projects from which the quilt pieces were probably leftover scraps, or the discarded dresses, shirts, or blouses from which they may have been scavenged. Let the images that form in your mind's camera develop into one or more word pictures. Then use the word picture(s) to write a poem or an essay.

Rummaging Through the Attic

When my husband and I added a room to our modest home, we gained storage space, both in the new room and in the extended basement beneath it. So as soon as the addition was complete, he climbed into the attic and handed down everything that had been stored there for the past twenty years. There was an old mantle clock without a key, a set of air horns from our 1960 *Chris Craft* cruiser, a copper and glass ice bucket shaped like a ship's lantern, a set of brown and yellow pottery we had purchased on a hillside in France, in 1964, and several more items that had to be sorted, repacked, or tossed.

Every item, or group of items, sparked a vivid image of how and when it had been acquired, used or not used, and finally stored away. Among the most-used were toys that had survived my sisters' and my growing up—especially the table and chairs our dad had built, the doll-sized couch our mother had made, and the kid-sized wicker rocker she had upholstered to match the couch. Then there was the toy cash register; the pink, blue, and green pastel glass tea set that always went to my sister's and my outdoor pretend playhouse; my *Toni* doll, with hair curlers, *Toni* solution, and handmade clothes; and the *Effanbee* doll whose fingers and toes still sported small bandages made of adhesive tape.

Just as precious, though, were our son's favorite childhood toys: the Jack-in-the-Box that always refused to jump out of the box, and the small green tractor with its still-bent axles, which he played with in the sand beneath the Chinese elm that once stood outside our kitchen window.

❖ Getting the Picture
From a closet, or an attic, find any *scrap* from the past, preferably one that stirs your emotions. It could be an article of clothing, a hat, a pair

of shoes, a purse, a tobacco pipe, or the like. Let the images of touch, smell, and sound that form in your mind's camera develop into one or more word pictures that describe the item and the person to whom it belonged. Then use the word picture(s) to write a poem or an essay.

Turning the Kaleidoscope

Shortly *before* my mother died, she gave me a quart-sized, blue *Ball* canning jar filled with half of the buttons she'd been saving in a sewing box since the time she and my dad were married. While I'd always known Mom saved buttons from old shirts, skirts, etc., I had never looked closely enough to see that the box held a great deal more than buttons.

Now, as I rotated the jar, and then emptied its contents onto the table, I could only "ooh" and "aah" as vivid images of my childhood spilled into my mind's camera. The fact that Mom had saved what most mothers would have thrown away overwhelmed me nearly as much as the trinkets I found in the jar. And my sister was just as pleased with her half of the button jar mix.

The Button Jar

Except for simple mending jobs,
I never paid much mind
To buttons, snaps, or fasteners
Of any shape or kind;
In fact, I'd always thought the button jar
Was just Mom's way
Of saving buttons I deemed useless
For a rainy day –
Until the day I tipped it and
Familiar trinkets spilled
From every inch of space that they
Had fallen to and filled.

It seems, while we were growing up,
That jar had been Mom's store
For things retrieved from pockets or
Just picked up off the floor.
Among old leather buttons were
Matched buttons strung on threads
And single buttons still attached
To bits of clothing shreds;
But strewn among them all, reminders
Of a younger time:
Play money, minted *Uncle Sam*—
A quarter and a dime;

A brown-toned wooden cherub sporting
Coats of old shellac;
Three solitary checkers,
Nineteen fifty's vintage, black;
A rusted metal butterfly;
A bauble from a shoe;
A souvenir medallion dated

Nineteen fifty-two;
A dainty rhinestone bracelet wound
Around and in between
The remnant of an earring and
A copper chain, turned green.

Though the button jar may not appeal
To the average person's eye,
For me it holds a wealth of treasures
Money cannot buy.

After Mom died, I found another myriad of her own trinkets that she had saved and that I didn't know what to do with but couldn't bring myself to throw away. As they began to pile up, I thought of the blue button jar Mom had given me. Why not use a similar jar for Mom's trinkets? Back home, I picked out a blue, half-gallon *Ball* jar that had been Grandma's and filled it with everything from loose macramé beads to casino tokens Mom had carried home in her pocket. When one jar wasn't enough, I reached for another.

Each of what I now call my "memory jars" holds a kaleidoscope of shapes and colors that can be tumbled and ogled over, or its contents dumped out onto the floor, to be picked up, held, and scrutinized. But I didn't stop there. I also gathered up small items of my dad's, including the paper punch from his childhood paper route, and filled another jar. Since then,

I have been filling jars with my own trinkets, as well as my husband's, and our son's.

Whenever I find small odds and ends that I don't know what to do with, they go into our respective memory jars. I am still in the process of writing about those jars.

❖ Getting the Picture

Find (or buy) a special jar and reserve it for loose trinkets that you want to keep but don't really know what to do with. As the jar begins to fill up, let the images that form in your mind's camera develop into one or more word pictures describing some of the trinkets, telling how old they are and to whom they belonged. Then use the word picture(s) to write a poem or an essay.

Chapter 4

Walking Back Through Time

Uncovering Pathways

Several summers ago, when I came within walking distance of the house where my two older sisters and I were raised, I got the overwhelming urge to retrace our steps on the sidewalks where we had walked to Lincoln School every day of our elementary lives. Without another thought, I walked vigorously to "our" house, where "our" gigantic white mulberry tree still stood in the back yard.

Then I deliberately slowed down and walked on up the street to the corner where the street meets a small park, where the sidewalk still begins, and where every crack and buckle took me back to those days when we tried not to break our mother's back and still get to school early enough to jump rope or play jacks with our respective girlfriends before the first bell rang.

Images crept into my mind's camera as, once again, I imagined Mom and my sister walking to school with me that very first day; as I felt the chill of rainy days when we wore boots and carried umbrellas (or not); and as, once I reached the schoolyard, I mentally stepped into the long narrow cloakroom that I knew was nestled between the first and second grade rooms. Several years before, images of that cloakroom, lined with pint-sized coats and boots and umbrellas, had formed in my mind's camera and inspired a 400-word story poem called "Priscilla's Pink Umbrella."

That story appeared in a 1984 issue of *Children's Playmate* magazine. Eleven years later, when I was invited back to what had been sold and converted into a church school, I had the honor of presenting contest awards to aspiring young writers and of reading my cloakroom-inspired story in the same auditorium that had intimidated me as a first-grader.

Now I stood at one corner of the old playground, wishing that my sister could be there to reminisce with me. The fact that I followed two years behind her, usually with the same teachers, and in the same classrooms, had made things difficult for me at times. I was expected to be as perfect and as smart as she was. But that simply wasn't the case. And I'm quite sure that she never had to stand in the corner, like I did in third grade, over my flat-out refusal to peep like a chicken during our story reading circle.

The Corner

The corner was the place
where thoughts ended
and began again
and pride took its stand
before colliding head-on
with humility.

One sister had already graduated from high school, and the other had moved on to junior high, when our school suffered a horrible tragedy that brought images crashing into my mind's camera on yet another day when I went back to photograph the nooks and crannies of our old playground.

Tallying the Loss

Her sallow shades pulled to half mast,
she sleeps amid islands of asphalt that
soak up the sun; dreaming, no doubt,
of days when leaf-filtered rays
played on graveled grounds
and little girls' voices chanted the

cadence of rhymes set to
hopscotch and double Dutch—
voices stilled the day
an early bell
shortened
recess
and
shades were pulled to their limits as
pupils were herded across hallways,
away from the side where
a limb had snapped and
snuffed out a life.

In the weeks that followed,
lumbermen worked frantically
to cut the memory of that day
from every schoolyard in town.

❖ Getting the Picture

Go to your old neighborhood, if possible, and retrace the steps you took getting to school when you were a youngster. Take along a camera and snap some photos of anything you find that has *not* changed, e.g. the school building itself, the trees you played under, the playground, etc. Let the images that form in your mind's camera develop into one or more word pictures describing (1) how the neighborhood and school have changed, or not; and/or (2) the *first* firsts in your life, such as your first day of school, your first teacher, your first day away from home without your parents. Then use the word picture(s) to write a poem or an essay.

Taking the Lid off the Kettle

The path we took to school each day was the same path Mom walked to get to Grandma's house every Wednesday, to clean. Wednesday was a special day for us, too. Instead of walking home for lunch, we got to walk to an aunt's house, near the school, for lunches of tomato soup or hot tamales, or to Grandma's house, for lunch with her and Mom. At the end of the school day, we'd walk to Grandma's house again, to meet Mom and wait for Dad to pick us all up.

Pass the Onions, *Please!*

Grandma often made potato
Soup for us for lunch,
With lots of onions that still had
A little bit of crunch.
And we loved Grandma's cooking but
Assured her that, no doubt,
Her soup would be much better if
She'd leave the onions out.

And then one day, when Grandma served
Her hot potato soup,
We took our spoons and stirred and sipped
The milky broth, but—*OOPS!*
It didn't taste like Grandma's soup;
We both were sure of that.
How could it be that Grandma's soup
Could taste so dull and flat?

We dilly-dallied over lunch,
Still sipping as we stirred,
And through it all, we noticed Grandma
Didn't say a word.
But from the look on Mother's face
We knew, without a doubt,
That Grandma had deliberately
Left all the onions out.

Now we assured her that her soup
Was really not *that* bad,
But as we headed back to school,
We both felt need to add
That when we came to Grandma's house
To eat her soup again,
We'd probably like it better if
She'd leave the onions in.

Grandma's kitchen always smelled of something baked, especially pies. So it was easy to record images of her kitchen table covered with flour and dough, and to sift word pictures, and then a poem, from those images.

Under Grandma's Spell

I don't recall the reason or
How old I was the day
Mom dropped me off at Grandma's house,
All by myself, to play.
I do remember, though, how Grandma
Taught me how to spell
My name, and how to write it out;
And I remember well

That I could not remember how
The letter "L" should sound,
And how I ran to Grandma every
Time I wrote it down;
How Grandma's floured rolling pin
Fit in her floured hands;
And Grandma's table, loaded down
With fillings, dough, and pans;
And how she'd roll her pie dough out
And pour the filling in
While helping me to sound aloud
The letter "L" again.

While I don't recall ever seeing Grandma refer to a recipe, some of her favorite and best dishes ended up on cards in Mom's recipe file. The following Japanese kyoka, which requires no title, best describes how I felt about that recipe file.

her recipe file
I put dibs
on the card
that's smudged
and faded

❖ Getting the Picture
Find an old cookbook, or an old recipe, preferably one of your grandmother's or your mother's, and prepare a dish that you enjoyed as a child. As you gather the ingredients, notice the condition of the book or recipe. Is it well

used? Are there smudges made by hands that were forever cooking or baking? Let the images that form in your mind's camera develop into one or more word pictures describing the cookbook, the person who used it, aromas that must have come from her kitchen, and how the dish you're preparing from it might compare in taste to when you ate it as a child. Then use the word picture(s) to write a poem or an essay.

Untying the Apron Strings

We rarely saw Grandma without an apron covering her housedress. In fact, nearly every *snap*shot we have of her shows her in an apron — even with her coat on, when she was on her way to helping out with a Lodge supper. Among the *scraps* of materials Mom had stored away in the steamer trunks, to cut into quilt pieces someday, was a 35¢ *Simplicity Printed Pattern* for a large apron. From the tattered envelope, and the pinking-shear-cuts on the pattern pieces, I knew it was the very pattern Mom had revamped and used as a guide to make every apron I ever saw Grandma wear.

Apron Strings and Angel Wings

I remember Grandma's cooking and
Her cherry pies but, more,
I remember Grandma's nature and
The aprons that she wore.
For it seemed whatever Grandma did,
From the time she rose at dawn
Till the time she went to bed at night,
She had an apron on.

Grandma never had much money for
A lot of fancy things,
So for years Mom sewed her aprons, all
Complete with bibs and strings.
Grandma liked those handmade aprons, though
Somehow I always thought
That she might have rather had a gift
That Mother could have bought.

But the years taught me that Mother knew
A great deal more than I,
For her stitches held a kind of love
That money could not buy;
And the aprons that she sewed each year,
Whether flowered, striped, or plaid,
Helped to bind the mother-daughter ties
That Mom and Grandma had.

Now an apron holds no magic, so
It cannot guarantee
That the one who wears it will become
What a mother ought to be;

But the mother who can put it on
And be thankful for its need
Is the mother who puts magic into
Every thought and deed.

And, although her apron pockets held
No treasures she could share,
Grandma's long, and somewhat tattered, apron
Strings were always there.
Now, when Mother wears an apron, it's
Through childlike eyes I see
Just how much she favors Grandma in
The ways that count with me.

Surely God gives every mother tasks
That she alone can do,
And if she has faith to ask His help,
Her troubles will be few.
But before He fits each mother with
A pair of angel wings,
He'll make sure that she has passed the test
In a pair of apron strings.

❖ Getting the Picture

Think back, to a special pocket in your past, one of a grandmother, a parent, or an aunt or uncle, that might have held a special or secret treat for you: a stick of gum, a piece of candy, a few pennies, a nickel, or a dollar. Let the images that form in your mind's camera develop into one or more word pictures describing how you felt about that pocket and the anticipation of finding out what was in it. Then use the word picture(s) to write a poem or an essay.

❖ Getting Around Town

Grandma lived just two blocks south of downtown. Since she didn't drive, she often walked to the Piggly Wiggly grocery store and the meat market, both of which were in the same block of Pekin's main street. Memories of one such walk with her left me with images dancing through my mind's camera — images that didn't get developed until many years later.

Grandma and the Carousel

The carnival set up the day
I went to Grandma's house to stay
And, hand in hand, I walked with her
Amid the tantalizing whir.
They'd shut the town down, roped and barred
The streets around the old courtyard,
And barkers called from booths and tents
Alive with cotton-candy scents.
The Ferris wheel spun in the sky,
But wooden ponies caught my eye;
The hollow-pitched calliope
Puffed playful tunes that beckoned me.
Then Grandma stopped and stood a spell
Right by the dancing carousel;
She seemed at once to understand
And slipped a nickel in my hand.

The ponies slowed, then settled down.
I headed straight for one nut-brown,
But as I fumbled for the rein
A younger hand grasped at the mane;
The ground beneath my feet gave way,
The nut-brown pony raced a gray,
And mothers clung to ponies' sides,
Intent on giving babies rides.

As laden ponies galloped off,
Then circled back to chide and scoff,
I sank into a horse-drawn seat
Lest I should forfeit Grandma's treat.
Sensations of enchantment fled
Like myths o'back each thoroughbred,
And Time combined her wile and wit
To break my spirit, bit by bit.

Neath painted hooves, gay tunes were lost.
The nickel that the ride had cost
Was gone! and through the wooden maze
I caught a glimpse of Grandma's gaze.
Outside the gate, she strained to see
Which playful pony carried me,
And from her countenance I knew
She sensed the disappointment, too.

As brazen pipes ran low on steam,
I stumbled past my halting team
And walked back home without a sound;
But in my trampled thoughts I found
That wooden ponies could not weigh
Against the bond I felt that day,
For Grandma found no need to tell
Of my ponyless ride on the carousel.

❖ Getting the Picture

Go to a carnival and ride the carousel! Let the images that form in your mind's camera develop into one or more word pictures describing the sights and sounds around you, including the expressions on the ponies' faces and the delight (or not) in their eyes at carrying you and their other passengers. Then use the word picture(s) to write a poem or an essay.

Looking Up the Facts

Our town's public library was also within walking distance of home. It was just a block over from Grandma's house, in fact, and once I became acquainted with it, it became one of my favorite getaways. By the time we started going there, I was almost too old for the children's department. But I remember the anticipation, and the satisfaction, of searching for books downstairs while my sister was upstairs, in the "big people's" department. And even after I started going up to *that* department, I longed to go back downstairs, without looking conspicuous, just to browse around.

I still feel that magnetic pull toward the children's department, in our relatively new library. I credit that pull with giving me the inspiration to write some eighty children's stories, poems, and puzzles for *Turtle*, *Children's*

Playmate, *Jack and Jill*, *Child Life*, and *Humpty Dumpty's* magazines (all publications of the Children's Better Health Institute, The Benjamin Franklin Literary & Medical Society, Inc.).

Our old library was demolished decades ago and its beautiful brick and stone hauled away. But the fact that the building itself is gone doesn't mean that I can't go back to it with my mind's camera and climb the cold stone steps that readied me for the complete and utter silence, and the overwhelming smell of aging paper and book bindings, that closed in around me when I stepped inside. Unlike the noisy library of today, from the second the doors closed behind us, the only accepted sounds were those of footsteps and *whispered* requests for help from the librarian.

The Old Library

It was one of the few places
I preferred to go alone: an
inner sanctum of mystery and suspense,
where the sound of my own footsteps
closed in around me; where I'd slip past
the towering wooden desk,
glimpsing only the plump torso of the woman
who held hoards of information between
two long black braids twisted in pinwheels
on either side of her head
and who, alone, judged whether or not
a laugh, or a whisper, or the

scarfing of chair legs on the marble floor
was too loud or too harsh; and
where I could lose myself
between the stacks, in the
quiet smell of aging pages and
leather bindings that left
a powdery residue on my fingers
and a keen sense of adventure
in my soul.

❖ Getting the Picture

Go to your favorite library and linger between the stacks, touching the books, reading their titles, and taking in the smell of their bindings and paper. Let the images that form in your mind's camera develop into one or more word pictures describing a library experience, good or bad, that you had as a child. Then use the word picture(s) to write a poem or an essay.

Chapter 5

Taking Shortcuts

Cutting through the Alley

No grass ever grew beneath the lilac bushes that lined the alley side of our back yard and offered plenty of shade for kittens to hide on sultry days. But leaves weren't enough to hide my sister and me the day we snatched up one of Dad's smoldering cigarette butts, just to see what it was like to smoke. What we didn't realize was that Mom always had an eye on us. In fact, from our kitchen window, she had a bird's eye view of everything in our back yard, including the lilac bushes and whatever, or whoever, was hiding in their shade.

Under the Lilacs

That day, our hearts
pounded in unison as we waited
for Dad to toss the smoldering

remains of his cigarette
onto the cinder alley before
going inside to kiss Mom hello.
Then we scarfed up the loot and
scooted to the ungrassy spot
where the kittens hid,
nudging them aside lest their
constant mewing give us away.
But hardly had we tasted
those last bitter puffs than
we saw Dad's feet planted
firmly on the alley side;
and when we emerged,
the look on his face was all
we needed to hear.

The alley was our link to neighbors' yards on the other half of our block — one that had a garage Dad rented, the winter before he built ours; and one that had a real playhouse that we could see from our back yard. The playhouse was probably a whopping 6' x 9', with a doorway in one end and pane-free window openings the rest of the way around. Telltale signs of green paint and whitewash filled the weathered lines of its tongue and groove siding. More importantly, though, the narrow windowsills, and built-in benches that lined its inside walls, provided perfect ledges for drying mud pies.

The Real Thing

It made no sense to us
that a tomboy should have
a whole basement full of dolls,
with buggies and cradles,
blankets, bottles, and chairs,
and pink squeeze bottles of
real baby lotion and
real baby oil
for the rubber parts of the doll
that looked and felt and smelled
like a real baby to us; or that,
across the alley, in her back yard
a real playhouse with
pane-less windows and
benches all 'round
should stand idle except for days
when we swept it clean and
used its benches for
drying mud pies,
never minding that the next time
she'd ask us over to play,
we'd find those pies
broken and scattered
and ready to be
swept up again...

❖ Getting the Picture
Go to an area of a small town where alleys still divide residential blocks. Walk or drive at least one length of an alley. Take special note of the back yards that line both sides of it, and

how they are being used: for storage of items people don't want seen from the street? for work projects (automotive, etc.) that can't be done on the street? or for children's play areas and family get-togethers? How does any one of them compare to a back yard in your childhood? Let the images that form in your mind's camera develop into one or more word pictures. Then use the word picture(s) to write a poem or an essay.

Steeling the Nerves

Warnings about how to handle raw poultry came long after the days we spent at Grandma's after she moved outside of town, cleaning what seemed like hundreds of chickens, for freezing, and long after our feelings had been steeled by the sights and sounds of our own neighbor lady's killing and dressing chickens she had raised, right across the alley from us.

Sunday's Chickens

It was always *Mrs.* A who
ran them down and
lopped off their heads with the
axe she kept buried in the
tree stump near the garbage pit—
right there in the middle of
the block, where her back yard

faced ours—before she
strung them up to drip dry
from the same lines
where she'd
hang her wash,
come Monday.

At Grandma's, the killing of the chickens was always over by the time we arrived with an aunt who drove us and our cousins there in a pickup that sometimes struggled to make it up the hills along the way. By that time, water for the scalding was already heating over an open fire, and double rinse tubs were already filled with cold water, for the washing.

The work for our moms started as soon as all the aunts and cousins had arrived. While some scalded the carcasses and picked them free of feathers that clung to fingers, others stood prepared to cut, and still others, to wash.

While my sister and our cousins played Red Rover and Hide 'n' Seek, I preferred to squeeze in beside Mom and reach to the very bottoms of the rinse tubs, through water already putrid with blood and grit and fatty scum, to retrieve the gizzards and rinse them free of corn and sand.

It was in that same timeframe, I believe, that my sister and I began to realize what the killing of animals really meant. As the son of a fisherman and hunter, Dad was proficient in both sports. But he totally gave up hunting the day we saw him shoot a rabbit and ever after accused him of killing Bugs Bunny.

❖ Getting the Picture
Think back, to a task or chore you were given (or took on) as a child, that haunts you yet today. Let the images that form in your mind's camera develop into one or more word pictures. Then use the word picture(s) to write a poem or an essay.

Pedaling Up the Street

Willow Park was appropriately named for one of the three streets that bordered its elongated, triangular shape. But it was dubbed "The Little Park" by those of us who either couldn't pronounce Willow, or who thought the park had been named for its size. Since it was only two blocks up the street, my sister and I would get there on foot, or on the oversized trike we shared—one manning the pedals and handlebars, the other standing firmly on the back platform, with fingers digging softly into the driver's shoulders. Mom always knew where we were, and the neighborhood was so quiet that we could hear her calling from the curb if she wanted us home before our allotted time was up.

Summer brought activities to the park, led by area teachers who volunteered to organize games and crafts. Softball and box hockey were free but, for a quarter or fifty cents, we could string plastic beads; lace a lanyard, a belt, or a wallet; or pour plaster into rubber molds and paint them the following day, once they had dried. At the end of the week, there was usually a costume parade or, better yet, a pet parade. Years later, some of those images marched into my mind's camera and became lines in a poem for one sister's birthday.

Keepsakes and Trinkets

Keepsakes and trinkets and 'kid' souvenirs
Recapture reflections of long-ago years;
But only the times of which love was a part
Can summon the memories locked in a heart.
And scenes of one's childhood are greater, by far,
For sisters who've turned out as close as we are.
So, Sis, on this birthday, I'm sure you'll agree
That love makes these memories as dear as can be:

Dressing up kittens for animal shows;
Walking to town; playing under the hose;
Riding our trike to the neighborhood park;
Capturing fireflies long after dark;
Jump-rope and hopscotch and skating on walks;
Stale penny-candy and 'little girl' talks;

Mud-pie concoctions we baked in the sun;
'Soups' made of elm seeds and water and fun;

Sharing the whooping cough, measles and mumps;
Being elated or down in the dumps;
Draping Mom's clotheslines with blankets, for tents;
Buying a turtle for twenty-five cents;
Dragging our 'playhouse' equipment outside;
Taking our dolls when we went for a ride;
Guarding each other, no matter the cost;
Sharing a skate key because one was lost;

Making up songs that were clever, we thought;
Jumping on beds till we finally got caught;
Walking to Sunday School; singing duets;
Trading our bracelets and favorite barrettes;
Secrets we vowed that we never would tell;
Getting to school just ahead of the bell;
Building fond memories that happiness brings;
Never forgetting our favorite things.

Though scenes of our childhood took place long ago,
Each parcel and circumstance helped us to grow;
And time has not altered the way that we feel,
For each priceless moment was precious and real.
So treasure each moment, the first to the last,
For much of the present is linked with the past,
And days without memories soon fade away,
But a childhood like ours is as clear as today.

❖ Getting the Picture

Think back, about a favorite park you enjoyed going to as a child. Let the images that form in your mind's camera develop into one or more word pictures describing the park itself, who took you there, and what you enjoyed most about the adventure(s). Then use the word picture(s) to write a poem or an essay.

Shaking the Piggy Bank

Our block had one sidewalk along its east side, while the block to the north of us had two sidewalks that met on its southeast corner. Together, the sidewalks across the street led to the general store around the corner, where we bought candy and soda pop and the few things Mom occasionally needed between grocery days.

Journal Entry: The General Store

"It was a wood frame building on a block foundation, with a wooden porch that echoed the footsteps of potential customers, and a tiny bell above the door that jingled at the slightest jar.

Inside, a crowded arrangement of goods and articles lined both sides of a wide "path" that led directly to the glassed-in meat counter. To the left, a wooden counter held the cash register and a large roll of brown paper; to the right, a barred postal window stood half-hidden behind shelves of merchandise that we never had occasion to buy.

Mr. B—who was owner, sales clerk, and postal clerk, all in one—worked from narrow aisles between the counters and shelved walls that were stocked clear to the ceiling. On the upper shelves were "unmentionable" items, like *toilet paper*, that we were too embarrassed to *ask* for, that Mom had to write notes for, and that could only be reached with a claw-like pole that opened and closed with a squeeze of the handle.

In front and to the left of the sales counter, there was a soda machine—the kind where bottles had to be fished out of chipped ice and water. And later, a newer model that dispensed one bottle at a time, from metal tracks that kept the bottles suspended in cold water.

After choosing a flavor by its cap—*OSO Grape, Dad's Root Beer, Orange Crush, or Lemon Lime*—the bottle had to be slid to the end of the track, where it could only be released by inserting a nickel in the coin mechanism.

To the left of the door, in front of the window, a slanted glass counter held shelves jammed with open boxes of penny candy. But merchandise was usually stacked in front of the counter, so Mr. B. would let us step into the aisle behind it, to decide how we'd spend our pennies. That sometimes took a while, yet we usually ended up with the same things—a thin, black box of licorice cigarettes "rolled" in white paper (until the day we got them home and found them crawling with worms); wax lips; and an authentic-looking, white-with-pink-lettering box of sugar cigarettes with pink "glowing" ends.

Any remaining pennies went toward *Double Bubble* bubble gum or, on days when we really felt like splurging, *Pink Owl* cigars. Then we'd walk back home, to sit on the curb and "smoke" while we decided what we were going to do next."

After a guided freewriting session describing everything I could remember about that store, and then transferring those notes to my journal, it wasn't difficult to put the facts in poetry form.

Mr. B's General Store

We seldom shopped there for
anything other than candy or soda pop,
unless Mom forgot something
at Piggly Wiggly or the A & P,
and then it was usually
something that we didn't want to ask for
and that required a note we could

hand to Mr. B, who was owner, sales,
and postal clerk all wrapped into one.
If he didn't hear our footsteps on
the wooden porch, he never
missed the jingling of
the bell on the door.
And if our note said *toilet paper*,
he'd reach with a long pole
to bring down a roll from a top shelf;
but if all we wanted was candy or soda,
he'd let us step behind the counter
to help ourselves.

His soda machine held nickel bottles
suspended in ice water by their necks
so that we had to choose the flavors by
their caps—*OSO Grape, Dad's Root Beer,
Orange Crush, Strawberry, Lemon Lime...*

The glass shelves of his candy counter
were jammed with cardboard trays of
penny candies (and some that ranged
from two cents to a dime); and though we'd
linger over what our pennies and nickels
could buy, we always ended up with
two packs of cigarettes—
white sugar ones with pink *glowing* ends,
and black licorice ones wrapped in
thin white paper.

Back on our own curb, we'd discuss
all that lay within the boundaries
of our young world, while puffing
on cigarettes that burned
nothing more than

candy counter musings
into our hearts and souls.

❖ Getting the Picture
Think back, to the main grocery store in your childhood, whether it was a general store, a supermarket, or a convenience store. Then think of your favorite item that came from that particular store. Let the images that form in your mind's camera develop into one or more word pictures describing the store, who took you there, and what they bought (or didn't buy) for you. Then use the word picture(s) to write a poem or an essay.

Skating Around the Block

Getting to the general store posed no problem for us. We usually chose to walk, even though we had two other modes of transportation—our trike and our skates. While the trike was mostly reserved for trips to the park, our skates were mostly reserved for continuous trips up and down the sidewalks across the street, when we didn't have to remove them until we were ready to walk back home.

On skates, we moved swiftly along to the rhythm of steel wheels whirring on the concrete, accompanied by the steady beat of expansion cracks, and interrupted only by an occasional break in both sounds, wherever tree roots buckled the sidewalk and we had to step over them to keep from tripping.

By the standards of today's inline skates, our roller skates had only one greater advantage: they grew as we did, sliding open, with the help of a skate key, to clamp onto the soles of our shoes, no matter what the size.

Getting Around the Block

We called it "skating around
the block," although
getting *all the way around* it
was impossible, for the
sidewalk only went halfway,
and we were only allowed to skate
as far as it went.

The sidewalk offered
challenges to be conquered;
left imaginations tingling as we
took the steep slants of driveways in stride
and bridged gaps and caverns
where restless roots of
hackberries and elms
undermined whole sections of the walk
and caused them to heave and buckle,
as if miniature earthquakes
had hit there at one time
or another.
Little could we know that
life itself is undermined

with do's and don'ts
and wills and won'ts,
and that once we
remove our skates,
the tingling only lasts
till we get back
across the street,
back to reality.

❖ Getting the Picture
Think back, to your main mode of transportation when you were a kid: a tricycle, bicycle, skates, or scooter? Let the images that form in your mind's camera develop into one or more word pictures describing your days aboard those wheels. Then use the word picture(s) to write a poem or an essay.

Chapter 6

Exploring the Waters

Tackling the Routine

My back-to-school "What I Did on My Summer Vacation" essays were as predictable as Dad's fishing reservations, on the same Minnesota lake, at the same time every year. The trip was so routine that I sometimes wonder why we always looked so forward to it. But we thoroughly enjoyed roughing it, right down to accompanying each other to the outhouse after dark, in order to discourage black bears that might be lurking in the woods, and pumping water into galvanized buckets whose granite or aluminum dippers had been used by everyone else before us.

Those highlights were further complemented by cabins with wood-burning stoves and wall-mounted kerosene lamps, genuine ice boxes for which blocks of ice were delivered every few days, riddled screens that offered little escape from persistent mosquitoes, and skunks that pilfered our garbage and sent horrific odors filtering up through wooden floors in the middle of the night.

Anticipation of the trip itself was heightened by preparations that involved the entire family, mainly, getting the car ready and then getting us, and it, packed. For as long as I could remember, Dad traded at a gas station owned and operated by a long-time friend named Sam, who always had a smile on his face and a shop rag dangling from his back pocket. Sam never failed to check the oil and wash the windshield while the gas tank was filling, or to pull that shop rag from his pocket and wipe his hands once the filler hose was back in its bracket. But the real fun for my sister and me came when things weren't quite so routine.

The Grease Rack

Sam's was a full service station
with a clock in the window;
the smell of grease from
one end to the other; and
a hoist that jiggled us up,
to a bird's eye view of
his planked workbench and
the green and white pyramid
of Quaker State Oil
stacked against one wall.

In gray-upholstered bliss,
we'd sit with our dolls,
quiet as church mice,
moving only heads and hands
for games of *Tic-Tac-Toe* and
I Spy, content with the lull of
Dad's voice below and
disappointed only when
Sam jiggled us all
back down to earth.

Once the car was in good running order, it was time for the rest of us to pitch in and spend a day cleaning it. Because preparations for our summer vacations always followed the same pattern, images flowed easily into word pictures and then into poems.

The Old Gray Plymouth

Our old gray Plymouth had no shine;
Dad bought it new in thirty-nine
But never worried much about
The way it looked, inside or out,
Though once a year he'd pull that car
Right up into the yard so far
That neighbors all around the block
Would bow to curiosity and flock
To see that car lose grit and grime
Because it was vacation time.

Once armed with rags and garden hose,
We'd set to work as we each chose

The cleaning jobs that we liked best
And left the others to the rest.
We kids would climb inside and share
The whisk-broom dust that filled the air,
Then wipe off knobs and glass and dash
While Mom and Dad let water crash
In playful falls that splashed and ran
The dirt right off that old sedan.

We'd clean until our arms were worn
And polish till the rags were torn,
And by the time we were all through,
That old gray Plymouth looked brand new.
But, though it stole the show that day,
We knew it wouldn't stay that way,
For once our things were packed and stowed,
And once that car was on the road,
The dirt would build till next year, when
Vacation time rolled 'round again.

❖ Getting the Picture

Think back, to something that was routine about your childhood—something you could count on happening, good or bad, no matter what. Let the images that form in your mind's camera develop into one or more word pictures describing whatever you can remember about the routine and how it might still be affecting your life today. Then use the word picture(s) to write a poem or an essay.

Unpacking Adventures

By the time the car was ready, Mom had most of the packing done for all of us, right down to groceries that were either unavailable, or too expensive to buy, once we got to Minnesota. So all that was left was to find a place for hauling everything she had packed, as well as the five of us. Dad had shied away from using our luggage carrier for the roof after the year two men in a strange car tried to stop us by blocking the otherwise deserted two-lane road we were traveling. So everything had to go in the trunk or in the back seat, with us.

Leader of the Pack

As far as memory takes me back,
I liked to watch my mother pack
When school was out and summer found
Our family Minnesota-bound.
Dad always left the car the day
On which they'd planned our getaway,
And Mom would have it ready when
He got back home from work again.
She always spent a week or two
In planning, like good packers do—
In filling boxes, one by one
With everything beneath the sun;
Arranging them, all in a row
And knowing where each thing should go

And how the car would hold the load
For fourteen hours on the road.

But as the years passed, and we grew,
The things Mom had to pack did, too,
And she would cleverly decide
New ways to pack *us* for the ride.
With ice chests on the back seat floor,
She'd make a bed for two, but more,
Upon the window shelf would be
A comfy bed just right for me.

Then one year Dad got all upset.
How in the world could Mom forget
The most important thing to him!
And now, with packing space so slim,
He said there must be room for it,
Insisting it would surely fit
Between the boxes, neatly stacked
With everything that Mom had packed.

With neighbors looking on, they vied
With thoughts of changing things inside,
Which only led us to assume
We'd all end up with much less room
Or, worse, that when the sun went down
We'd still be in our own hometown.

So all the family got involved,
But it was Dad who finally solved
The puzzle, squeezing room enough
Inside the trunk with dolls and stuff,
By shifting those and clothes and food
To make room for the *Evinrude.*

Numerous images from our many seven-hundred-mile trips of family togetherness were still so clear in my mind's camera that I only had to sort them out before developing them into poems.

Highways from the Past

Before the interstates, when highways
Linked town after town,
And we'd get restless traveling, Mom
Knew how to calm us down:
She'd start a game of Alphabet
That no one could resist;
We'd move to our respective sides
So no signs would be missed,

And holler out the letters as
They showed, so all would know
How far ahead we'd gotten or
How far we had to go.
Whoever found them in their proper
Order first, would win,
And it got more exciting yet
When Mom and Dad joined in.

One sister'd take the driver's side,
With backward signs, for some
Were for the people who were heading
Where we'd just come from.
But I was confident to know
She didn't really mind,

For even if I pulled ahead,
She'd not be far behind.

Now A through P were snaps to find,
And, neck and neck, we knew
Whosever side got Quaker State
Could claim the Q through U;
And then, when faithful Burma Shave
Came into sight with V,
The only challenge left would be
To find X, Y, and Z -

Yet, should a town come into play,
Those letters were a breeze,
For little towns were blessed with street
And route signs, and marquees;
But just about the time we'd see
Our letters straight ahead,
Our route would veer and put them on
The other side instead.

Today's kids cling to handheld games
That pass the time away,
And parents don't get roped in, for
They're seldom asked to play;
And interstates save time by making
Travel smooth and fast,
But they don't leave impressions like
Those highways from the past.

Once all of the word pictures were recorded in my journal, the second poem came as easily as the first.

More Highways from The Past

When we were kids, the best of roads
Were only two lanes wide –
Two lanes that held a wealth of games
That kept us occupied;
So when we traveled anywhere,
We'd settle down to play
A game of Counting Cows that grazed
In fields along the way.

Each side had equal chances as
Cows showed up, left and right,
And all we had to do was count
The ones that came in sight.
One game could last forever or
Be over in a wink,
Depending on our counting skills
And if we paused to blink.

An estimate or guestimate
Was not a fair amount,
For we could only rightly claim
The cows that we could count.
A hundred cows, the goal; it wasn't
Very hard to do
As long as trucks or trees or billboards
Didn't block our view;

But either side that saw a graveyard
Where cows *could* have been
Was forced to bury all their cows
And start from scratch again;
Yet neither side dared scoff *or* cheer,

For sure as not, they'd find
A graveyard for *their* side was never
Lurking far behind.

Dad's theory was that the closer our cabin was to the lake, the quicker he could start fishing once we got there. And sure enough, no sooner had we unpacked the car and chosen our respective sleeping areas inside the cabin, than he was out on the back steps, rummaging through his tackle box for his favorite bass lure, assembling fly and casting rods, and carrying the outboard motor down to the wooden boat with our cabin number painted on its bow. In the years before he finally purchased a brand new *Evinrude* motor, he used an old outboard that may or may not run once he'd clamped it onto the transom.

Over a Barrel

Dad had a tendency to lean
Toward total dedication
In everything he did, including
Family vacation.
In fact, he got us hooked on making
Trips to Minnesota,
Where he would fish for days on end
To come up with his quota.
And he was fairly patient when
We'd try our skills at rowing,
Though sometimes we'd drift past the fishing

Hole where he was going.
But once he got an outboard that
Could get him fishing faster,
We found that any failure on
Its part could mean disaster,
Especially when conditions in
The weather were just right
For fishing which, to Dad, meant rain
Or shine or day or night.

Now getting from the cabin to
The lake was not a chore,
Though lugging back an outboard motor
Took a little more;
Yet every time it failed to start
We knew, without a doubt,
That he would bring that outboard up
The hill to check it out.
He'd clamp it to a heavy plank that
Spanned two tall birch trees—
Above a drum of water for
Emergencies like these.
He'd make a few adjustments then,
And deftly wrap the cord
And, with one pull, the thing would start,
Dad's confidence restored.

Light-footed and a little more
Lighthearted, he would tote
The outboard all the way back down
And clamp it on the boat.
But from our vantage point we'd hear
That outboard choke and sputter—
That, followed by a few choice words
He never failed to mutter.

Each time he'd bring the outboard up
And take it back again,
We'd think he might as well give in
And *row* the boat, but then,
His patience was more sure than ours,
And just when we'd begun
To think it was no use at all,
We'd hear that outboard run.

The first resort we went to, on Gladstone Lake, was one that Dad had found before he met Mom. Besides an even dozen kids, the owners had a springer spaniel that retrieved frogs from the moss at the lake's edge and brought them to us, unscathed.

One year, I teamed up with the youngest boy. We spent the better part of a week collecting dead fish that had washed up on the shore. Then we performed mass burials, walking over mounded graves, packing them down until putrid, yellow-green slime oozed out onto the sand. Only after my sister and the girl she palled around with declared their total disgust, did I realize that our project was not a very rewarding one.

There was a huge barn that held little more than baled straw and wild kittens we couldn't get close to, and a smaller barn where fishermen stored the quotas they planned to take home. In order for the game warden to determine those quotas, the fish could be gilled and gutted, but not beheaded. It was up to the fishermen themselves to place their unwrapped fish on blocks of ice inside the barn and cover them with sawdust that held in the cold. But one year the outside temperature soared, and every block of ice in the fish barn melted. We stood by as Dad scooped and buried a heaping wheelbarrow full of spoiled, sawdust-covered fish — an entire week's store that he and Mom had caught. The following year, we went to a newer resort on the same lake — one that had electricity in the cabins and an electric deep freeze in the office, for storing fish.

❖ Getting the Picture
Think back, about a trip you took with your parents, or someone else, when you were a youngster. Let the images that form in your mind's camera develop into one or more word pictures describing how you got to wherever you were going, who was with you, and what you did when you got there. Then use the word picture(s) to write a poem or an essay.

Fishing for Laughs

The newer resort had a hillside setting, with cabins not so improved that we weren't still roughing it all the time we were there. Its owners kept us in sight whenever Mom and Dad went out fishing by themselves. And they stood right beside us on the dock, sharing our anxieties, the day the wind whipped the lake into frothy whitecaps, and we couldn't see Mom and Dad's boat anywhere. Those images, described only in the word pictures of my journal, set the pace for the following poem.

The Dock

Its weathered planking jutted far enough
into the lake to secure the numbered
boats of the resort, but not far enough to
break up the whitecaps of summer
storms. Nevertheless, it was a safe haven
for live nets brimming with bluegill, and
stringers strung with largemouth bass.

It served as a springboard for the
russet-haired Vizsla who sailed through
the air to fetch sticks thrown
yards beyond her reach; as a meeting place
for fishermen who
had no time to visit on land; and as
our greeting spot when Mom and Dad
came in with their quota for the day;

so we sometimes forgot that
the slime of its underparts
harbored sleek black leeches
that clung for life to arms and legs and
only let go when we salted them down.

From a prized *snap*shot of Dad and me in rain gear, and me holding a stringer with three largemouth bass, I caught several vivid images of a very special day.

Fishing with Dad

Everyone knew that fishing with Dad
was an experience; but
fishing with Dad *alone* was an honor,
for his sole fishing partner
was usually Mom—except for the day
she opted to let me go in her place.

Daybreak found us heading out
to troll for walleye;
shutting the motor down;
coasting to the edge of a lily-pad field;
and me trying my hand at rowing quietly
while Dad let his fishing line trail behind.
But as the sun warmed the morning air,
we turned to casting for largemouth bass.

Back on shore, Mom mused over
the two-pounder I'd hauled in
while Dad stood smiling and
rocking up on his toes,
pretending he'd come in early
because of defeat.

Once in a while, Dad would hang up his fishing hat and drive us to the nearby tourist town of Nisswa, where Mom would pick up a few things from the small grocery store, then on to the souvenir shop, where we would linger over Indian dolls and turquoise rings. On one rare occasion, however, they left us at the cabin while they went to town, knowing that we were under the watchful eye of our older sister and the owners of the resort.

"Plum" Crazy

Before the days when grocers stocked
Fresh fruits abundantly;
Before the nectarine, when grapes
Were still a luxury;
The summer months brought favorites, and
Our groceries weren't complete
Till Dad had picked out several plump,
Red plums for us a treat.

And even when we went "up North"
To fish, we could rely
On Dad to see we always had
An ample plum supply;
But one year, while he did his best
To keep some on the shelf,
We plumb forgot our manners when
It came to Dad himself;

For Minnesota always found us
Freer, in a way,
And other people's kids were always
Coming 'round to play;
So, with the hospitality

That Mom and Dad had wrought,
It followed that we shared the red-ripe
Plums that they had bought.
Dad thought we'd gone "plum" crazy,
Though it didn't really dawn
On us that when *he* wanted one,
The plums were always gone.
Though he was seldom subtle
When we were in the wrong,
This time he "fought back" quietly,
And Mom played right along:

They left us at the cabin while
They went to town and back,
And with the groceries they brought in,
We spied a small, brown sack
That Dad left on the table and then
Waited, tongue in cheek,
To see how long our curiosity
Would take to peak;
And when it did, we saw the darnedest
Thing we'd ever seen,
For Dad had bought red plums all right,
But they were *all* plumb *green*.

❖ Getting the Picture

Think back, of a time when a parent or grandparent played a harmless practical joke on you. Let the images that form in your mind's camera develop into one or more word pictures describing the joke and how you handled it. Then use the word picture(s) to write a poem or an essay.

Tracking the Clues

One vacation netted us two Indian Chief *Paint-By-Numbers*, to work on when we were tired of swimming or catching frogs. The paintings were partially done, and still wet, when we laid them on top of the cold wood stove, where we were sure they would not be disturbed. But the next morning, the oil paint was smeared, and the unfinished areas were blotched with tiny, multi-colored footprints that trailed off across the top of the stove — clear evidence that the mouse we'd seen peering over the door sill the day before had checked out the paintings while we slept.

During one of our last Minnesota vacations, which took place before Dad started traveling for his work, tragedy struck the resort family with the twelve kids. A late-night boating accident claimed the life of their eldest son. When I finally got the urge to include the incident in my journal, I only had to turn to a back-to-school "What I Did on My Summer Vacation" essay for the details.

Excerpts from My 7th Grade Essay,
"Vacation of Excitement"

"...on the Tuesday night of the second week we were there, something happened which we all wish we could forget, but probably never will. Two boys, one nineteen, the other fifteen, were racing around the lake in a speedboat at about 9:30 p.m. They were acting silly and decided to ride the waves of another motorboat. Their boat tipped just enough to throw them out into the water, but the boat did not turn completely over.

The oldest boy had heavy boots and pants on, and when they got wet, he couldn't hold himself up. He couldn't swim very well anyway, so he drowned. The other boy, however, managed to keep himself up and called for help. The motor was still on all the way, and the boat kept right on going. By the time they [helpers] got there, they couldn't even find the other boy.

My mother and father had been fishing when all this happened. They heard a boat coming toward their own, and my mother turned the light on so that the people in the boat could see that they were there. As the boat went speeding by, about four feet from their boat, she shined the light in the bottom of the boat, and just about fainted when she saw that it was empty. If they had known what had happened, they could have made it in time to save both of the boys.

Instead, they thought someone was just acting silly, so they decided to chase the boat. They followed it until it finally ran into the bank. They then took the boat back across the lake, after shutting off the motor. When they were halfway across the lake, they met some men who told them what had happened. They were really sorry they hadn't gotten there sooner.

...they found the body two days later. They had been dragging the lake for a solid day. The next day there was a bad storm, and the body floated to the top."

While I had no *snaps* or *scraps* to rely on, *snippets* from the preceding essay, along with vivid details that had been seared into my mind's camera that year, set the mood for the following poem:

While Mothers Wait

I don't know why we went along with it,
the senseless things kids do
not to be left out of things, under
cover of night, slipping down to the
dock and into a boat, we, who
had not seen the sorrow death brings,
while a mother waited in torment.

In the sun's dwindling rays, boats had converged
like numbered lily pads, news echoing,
one to the other: the runaway boat had
beached itself on the far shore.
One boy rescued, they could only
speculate about the other, but knew too well
the cumbersome jacket and
work boots laced to their tops.

Now, the boys manned our oars,
deliberately silent so as not to raise
the living or the dead,
digging deep into rich black waters that
trickled back to the nothingness
we hoped was there; whispering tales that
sent chills rippling down our spines and
cut short each breath;
for what if, at daybreak, our boat was found
on the far shore...

Morning brought more volunteers
dislodging moss and lily stems where
largemouth bass loomed in darkness,
silent and tight-lipped.

Riding Out the Storm

Years later, two more water-related incidents ending in near tragedy left me with vivid and detailed images in my mind's camera. Enter: the present, and more recent events, where memories floated so near the surface that they only needed to be snagged and reeled in. No need for extensive searching or digging this time. The only tools needed were a few recent *snaps*hots, along with the *snippets* entered in my journal immediately after each incident happened. A combination of the two added more detail to what became essays and poems.

A Quiet Brush with Death

So this is the way it's going to end. Buried alive in churning waters. Headline to read: Illinois River Barge Claims Life of Forty-Year-Old Wife and Mother...but this is no ordinary river barge...

A few years prior, my husband Fred had found a deteriorating, nineteen foot steel-hulled tug boat nosed into the bank of a cooling water inlet no longer used by the power company where he was working; tied alongside it, a shop-crafted work barge made of v-shaped pontoons and quarter-inch plate steel. Formerly used for clearing the inlet of floodwater debris, both tug and work barge had sat idle for years. Maybe, just maybe, we could purchase them from the power company.

From the very day our bid was accepted, till the tug was safely moored in a marina ten miles north, Fred spent his lunch breaks trekking down to the inlet, first to dip rainwater from the tug's listing hull; later, to lug a new battery, spark plugs, or a few more gallons of fuel; or simply to turn the key, in hopes that the Chrysler flathead straight-eight engine would start.

When it never did, we paddled the tug out of the inlet and towed it upriver alongside our cruiser. In the meantime, with the help of a power company operator, and a cherry picker, Fred retrieved the work barge from its burial plot and placed it upside-down across the bed of our half-ton Chevy pickup. The barge spent a full summer in our back yard, undergoing repairs, before being transferred to the marina.

During the months that followed, Fred lived for the day we could outfit the tug to resemble the legendary *Merrimack*, complete with extended "iron" sides (in this case, heavy cardboard), and "cannons" (made of scrap pipe) that would spit confetti into the air, given a healthy blast of ignited oxygen. All of this *and* a shot at winning the morning phase of an annual river event that included two boat parades.

For the evening parade, we would transform the tug into a nostalgic paddle wheeler. The work barge would serve as the promenade deck, where three "Southern belles"—my mother, a friend named Sue, and myself—would sit at a table, sipping mint juleps to the tune of *Oh, Suzannah*.

By the time his goal became a reality, Fred had persuaded a carpenter on another job to build a scaled-down paddlewheel that would hang off the stern of the tug and turn with the force of its wake. But, since the tug's engine still wasn't running, a 25 horsepower outboard, mounted just ahead of the paddlewheel, would have to do, at least for the parades. In order to pilot the tug, Fred would squat on the back deck, behind the cabin. From there, he would be unable to see the path ahead. He would have to rely solely on the watchful eyes of his crewmates, namely, my stepfather and Sue's husband, for direction and instruction.

The morning parade went off without a hitch. We left a calling card of confetti floating on our mild wake as we headed back to the marina to change faces.

I sensed subtle hints of apprehension in Fred's voice as he checked and double-checked the steel cables that snugged the barge securely to the tug, against two steel uprights that served as bumpers. Tied together with two-inch-pipe crossbars, those uprights were the only obstruction between the barge platform and the deck of the tug.

More than once Fred looked at the barge and warned, "Keep an eye on the bow. If it starts to go down, jump onto the tug." I didn't have to ask why. Its platform set only inches off the water's surface, and we had never had a chance to test it under power. But the cables were taut, and the rest of the crew was ready to get underway. Nevertheless, I passed Fred's warning on to Mom, who, in turn, relayed it to Sue.

That balmy June night, we floated along under a soothing halo of blue lights strung from temporary poles on either side of the barge. Finding our place in line, we passed by the judges' boats, then cut away and headed back to the marina. There was still a short way to go when a small runabout angled across our path, from starboard to port.

I watched calmly, but intently, as the gentle beginnings of its wake spread toward us, gently lifting the starboard corner of the bow...gently letting it fall to catch the next battery of ripples that splashed playfully over the same corner and rolled back into the river as the bow lifted a little higher...dipped a little lower...caught a bigger swell...*then folded silently down, like a massive iron door closing slowly on its hinges*, the halo of blue lights trailing close behind...

"Get up!" I screamed, as chairs and table and all that they held slid forward and vanished into our swirling path. I spun around in time to sling one arm across my mother's back and hug her to the pipe cross-braces at the bow of the tug just as the barge dropped out from under us.

Sue's pleas to *"Stop!"* came from the deck of the tug and filtered off into the night; Mom's and mine trickled down the underside of the tug's tapered bow and spun away in its draft, stifled by the muffled din of the outboard.

Seconds drained away. The extreme limits of my reach began to take their toll. I heard the strain in my own voice: "I can't hang on much longer..." followed by the reassurance in Mom's: "I'm okay...let go of me and hang on..."

Letting go of the pipe on the other side of her would mean relying on the grip of one already strained hand, while bringing the other from at least a yard away, to reinforce it. But if I hoped to hang on any longer, I had no choice. Seconds later, my hands were side by side on the angled crossbar. The unexpected result was an additional arm's-length drop into the path of the tug and the now vertical barge. Both were pushing steadily forward, plowing me through the water with a force that glued my full-length denim skirt to the calves of my legs; the weight of it all tearing at numb fingers that were losing their grip on the cold steel...

...Mom was right. It is quiet when you get right up front, ahead of the engine. Thirteen years earlier, she had signed on as a maid on a commercial tow that transported oil up and down the southern leg of the Illinois River. At the time, Fred was working at a boiler house in the southern part of the state, so we were living on our cruiser, just a few miles from there. On mornings when "Mom's" tow passed by, on its way further south, she would walk out onto the bow of the front-most oil barge, to wave at us. *She was right. It's very, very quiet...*

Any semblance of strength, mingled with a dwindling will to hang on, trickled unrestrained from my fingers and swirled away in the muddy waters that tugged at my shoulders. Even when spurts of air bubbles rippled up my sides, I didn't sense the slowing...only the pressing away of water, from my armpits to my toes... and then the eerie lifting of the barge, resurfacing on its cable hinges, as slowly as it had gone down. At the same time, I felt Fred's hands on my ribcage, sensed his feet planted firmly on either side of my shoulders, and heard his reassuring, "I've got you!"

By the time he helped me to my feet, Sue was hugging Mom securely on the other side of the uprights, and her husband was retrieving my floating purse that had somehow stayed in the swirl of things.

Overlapping stories rang out in the darkness of the shorted-out halo of lights, now dripping with muddy river water. When I screamed, Sue had scrambled over the pipe bracing to the bow of the tug, dropped to her knees and clung desperately to Mom, who was still being shoved through the water, with me. Fred had thrown the outboard into neutral the second the other men hollered, *"The girls are in the water!"* not because they had seen us there, or heard our screams, but because the strings of blue lights had suddenly disappeared.

Next morning, in the calm of the marina, the cables that had stretched like rubber bands showed no signs of fraying *or* stretching. The only hint of our quiet brush with death came from still-wet clumps of river bottom mud that clung like gargoyles to the iron cleats of the barge's bow.

The other near-tragedy occurred in my early writing-and-getting-published days, when I felt I was too busy to keep a journal. In order to tell the story the way I wanted it told, I had to rely on *snap*shots I had taken, as well as *snippets* of information in letters I had written home. Following is that memory written first as an essay and then as a poem. Keep in mind that, just as events can be recorded in more than one genre, they can also be recorded in different forms within a genre. So don't squelch the urge to develop a memory in more than one way, should inspiration call for it.

From Riffles to Raging

It was the spring of 1983. With our son in college, and pipefitters' work in the Midwest at an extreme low, my husband Fred and I took our eighteen-year-old dachshund and headed for Alabama in a borrowed motor home. Our prayers were answered when Fred found work at a pipe mill that was under construction in Birmingham.

We spent the next six months just south of the mill, in a hillside trailer park situated between the Bessemer Super Highway and Valley Creek. Ours was the trailer pad nearest the creek and, once Fred left for work each morning, I'd spend a good portion of sunny days walking along, or sitting beside, the creek.

From its high bank, I took in the sights and sounds of shallow riffles that trickled toward deeper, shaded rock pools at the opposite end of the trailer park. On the far bank, between the riffles and the pools, hundreds of snapping turtles clambered up each morning and stacked themselves like toppled Dominoes, to bask on exposed tree roots.

Birmingham is not without its rainy season, however, and several times that summer the swollen creek swept through Bessemer, bringing debris—everything from hockey sticks to a dead dog—swirling past the trailer park.

One Sunday, while the creek was still running strong, we jumped into our VW and followed the course of it, just to see where everything would end up. A few miles down the line, we found a small iron bridge that had collected a vast array of basketballs, volleyballs, sneakers and boots. Thus Valley Creek became the fascinating subject of letters home, though little did we realize *how* fascinating.

It was the kind of morning that calls for going back to bed. A steady rain had fallen through most of the night. So as soon as Fred left for work, I cuddled up with the dog, listening to the patter of rain on the metal roof of the motor home, never dreaming of the catastrophe that was building outside.

Less than thirty minutes had passed when I heard the muffled sound of our VW, followed by frantic pounding on the door. My first thought was that Fred had been laid off. But when I opened the door,

I realized that wasn't the case at all. "Get ready!" he yelled above the drumming of the rain. "We have to get out of here!"

A glance in the direction of the creek answered the question that faded from my lips. The creek was out of its banks and was moving at horrendous speed. Fred slammed the door shut and started unhooking electrical cords. I threw on the clothes at hand and secured everything inside, including the dog.

In less than ten minutes, we were ready to move. But the creek wasn't waiting. It had already covered the only road that would take us to higher ground while edging its way up and over the trailer pad. Fred wheeled the motor home off the pad, into a swift current that washed the undercarriage and swirled sticks and debris past us, and around us, as we plowed through it.

There was not a soul in sight as we headed up the hill, parked the motor home on the incline, and locked the dog inside. By the time we ran back to get the VW, the rain was letting up, and neighbors had begun to appear from somewhere on the hill. Nevertheless, our trailer pad was totally covered with raging water still on the rise and threatening the undersides of trailers on higher ground.

Everything that was not tied down was moving. That's when it hit me—the realization that the motor home, with the dog and me in it, would have been swept down the creek, along with everything else, had Fred not come back when he did. But there was no time to linger on that thought; a whispered thank you prayer had to do.

While neighbors watched from the hillside, Fred and I waded into shin- and knee-deep water, rescuing lawn chairs, tables, and anything else that could be carried or dragged. A brand new motorcycle, cabled to a telephone pole, presented more of a challenge. Together, we half-walked, half-ran to the boat dealer at the top of the hill and borrowed a pair of bolt cutters. The cutters made short work of the cable and within minutes, Fred was walking the motorcycle to dry ground.

As we continued to wade in and out of the water, onlookers warned of electrical shock. However, it would be several weeks before I'd discover, while sitting alone beside the creek, that their real fears had stemmed from the fact that Valley Creek was home to water moccasins.

Once the rain stopped, the creek dropped back within its banks as quickly as it had risen, leaving mud and debris covering every inch of ground it had touched. Plastic bags, paper, and colorful remnants of clothing clung to branches of trees that lined the higher edges of the creek's bank.

Only then did it dawn on us that everyone who wasn't at work must have evacuated their trailers sometime in the night or early morning, but no warning had come our way. And only after my thoughts had time to settle did I turn to Fred and ask, "What *ever* made you come back?"

He said, "When I got to work, it was still raining, and something just told me I'd better head back and move the motor home away from that creek." We both knew what, or rather, *Who*, that "something" was.

Once the essay had been written, a poem wasn't far behind. While the poem contains basically the same information as the essay, I have included it here to show that it isn't necessary to stick to one genre when recording a memory. Which version to use where will ultimately be decided when yet another scrapbook, travelogue, or memoir starts coming together.

Valley Creek

What locals knew of Valley Creek, they
weren't telling. Even its name didn't
give it away, nor did lush green banks that
cradled the soothing ripple of
shallow rapids as they trickled toward
deeper, motionless pools shaded by
jutting rock ledges; and, between the
trickling and the stillness, hoards of
turtles clambering up to bask
on willow roots, their mud-green shells resting
one against the other, like toppled Dominoes.

So the betrayal was swift the day the rains came
and Valley Creek exploded, turning
swollen rapids loose to swipe its banks clean
of hockey sticks and dead dogs alike and
sweep them past us with a fury...only to
settle down minutes later, leaving shreds of
clothing and plastic bags dangling from branches,
like flags of surrender after a war.

We followed its course once, after
a rain; watched it sieve its way past
an iron bridge that hoarded a booty of
basketballs, volleyballs, sneakers and boots.
In August, strangers invaded the
creek bed, prodding for turtles already
burrowed down and hiding.

In August, catfish fell prey to the
cotton-white jaws of water moccasins
gliding silently about in the shadows.
But August came *after* the rains that lasted
all through the night and sent locals
scurrying to dry ground without so much
as a knock on our door, and us with
little time to rescue their belongings and ours
from cotton-rich waters.

❖ Getting the Picture
Go to a lake, a park lagoon, or even a creek. Sit near the water and observe any activity — people walking, children playing, ducks swimming, leaves floating on the surface of the water. Let the images that form in your mind's

camera develop into one or more word pictures describing the activity (or non-activity) in the area. Then use the word picture(s) to write a poem or an essay.

Flying Over the Sea

From teen age on, I've been blessed with travel, first with my parents, and then with my husband and son. On each of four extensive trips outside the States, I kept detailed journals, complete with *snap*shots, *scraps* (documents), and detailed *snippets* of information that I didn't want to forget. So yet another water scene came to life for me through *snap*shots and *snippets* gleaned from "*sPacific Wanderings*," a journal detailing the 1972-73 trip around the Pacific Rim. The following account, again in two different forms — in this case, free verse and a Japanese haibun — will be a reminder to our son of the eye-opening experiences he shared with us at age ten.

Lifeline of the City

March 1973 - Bangkok, Thailand:
In the half-light of dawn, our
curiosity piques with the racket outside, and
we scramble to windows overlooking a
maze of corrugated tin roofs on
a mud-brown canal where

sleek taxi boats transport scores of
white collar workers.

Later, we, too, are whisked along the
canal system and the Choa Phya River,
where children play aboard family junks
and small boats hang outboard of floating shops
laden with handmade baskets and clay pots,
hanging fabrics, and bundled bamboo.

Our gentle wake laps the steps of
tin shacks locked side to side, where
neither garbage nor debris hamper
dockside bathing, the washing of dishes and
laundry, or the brushing of teeth;
where fishermen work nets suspended
from bamboo poles, and old ladies paddle
boats weighed down with fresh produce,
dried fish, and bananas simmering atop hot coals;
and where brown-skinned boys tread
muddy waters to ambush our boat and
slam the satang we hand over
into their mouths before jumping back in,
to wait in ambush again.

At the Floating Market, where
blood mingles with brown river water,
a guide transfers German passengers
to our boat to make room for the boy who has just
tangled with his propeller.

In the afternoon sun, we
return from reality to swim in water
made clean and saved for tourists.

Again, while the preceding poem and the following haibun contain basically the same information, I will be using each of them in a different but appropriate scrapbook, travelogue, or memoir.

Main Stream Echoes

Wakened by clatter and chatter. We scramble to the only window in our room. Below, a maze of corrugated tin roofs and a mud-brown canal.

> Bangkok sunrise
> sleek taxi boats transport
> white-collar workers

Mid-morning. Tour guide navigates our low-riding boat along linked canals and through narrow channels umbrellaed by tropical overgrowth. A man cutting flowers hands one to me.

On the Choa Phya River, children play aboard family junks. Old ladies paddle boats weighed down with fresh produce, dried fish, and bananas simmering atop hot coals. Small boats hang outboard of anchored shops. Handmade baskets and clay pots; hanging fabrics; bundled bamboo.

> waterfront temple
> fisherman's net suspended
> from a bamboo pole

Steep river bank edged with garbage and debris. Tin shacks locked side to side. Dockside bathing; laundry- and dish-washing. Children stand waist deep, toothbrushes in hand. Brown-skinned boys tread water; climb aboard our boat and slam the satang we hand over into their mouths before jumping back in, to lie in wait. At the Floating Market, blood mingles with brown water: an "ambush" boy's toe severed by a propeller.

> afternoon sun
> we swim in clear water
> reserved for tourists

In any one of my travel journals, I can turn to a specific day of the trip and tell you where I was, what the weather was like, what I was doing, and who I was with. As a result, all of those journals are now being used to compile a complete travelogue that will ultimately become one more scrapbook, one more part of my memoirs. Yet that again poses the question of what a memoir should or should not be and what it should or should not include. As the writer of your own life stories, you alone can make those decisions.

No matter how you intend to write about and share your memoir, and no matter what memories you want it to include, it all comes back to having (or finding) memories to write about. Whether those memories are still close to the surface, or whether they have to be coaxed out with the use of *snaps, scraps,* and/or *snippets,* a journal of some kind is essential.

❖ Getting the Picture
Think back, to a long trip or a day trip, or any vacation you enjoyed with family or friends. Find a souvenir, or any *snap, scrap,* or *snippet* from that vacation and put it in front of you. Let the images that form in your mind's camera develop into one or more word pictures about the trip: what you liked or didn't like, and especially what made that trip more or less enjoyable than any other trip you have taken. Then use the word picture(s) to write a poem or an essay.

Chapter 7

Sifting Through the Sand

Bridging the Gaps

Summer Sundays usually found our family, plus Grandma and Grandpa, heading fifteen miles or so south of Pekin, to Spring Lake, which has since been established as a state fish and wildlife park. Mere anticipation made it seem more like a hundred miles to us. Outside the city limits, the roads were little more than one-lane paths and ruts, over hills comprised mainly of "blow sand," a name fitly given grains of sand rounded, shifted, and deadened by wind and time; grains that continually relocate themselves in areas where there are no windbreaks of hedge or evergreen.

Untreated at that time, the Spring Lake area yielded little in the way of produce, except for watermelon and cantaloupe, both of which were plentiful at several roadside stands along the way.

In the parking lot near the lake, we'd load up with the fishing gear Dad had brought, and the lunch Mom had packed, and make the long trek to what Dad considered the better fishing end of the lake. Single-file, we'd follow the sandy trails, dodging cow patties and prickly pears (dubbed "Spring Lake cactus" by anyone familiar with them) that sprawled in every direction. And sometimes Mom would lag behind with us, to pick wild gooseberries. But the rail-less wooden bridges that spanned what I can only describe as wide drainage ditches along the way always brought us to a complete standstill.

Built in the early 1900s, the bridges were made up of short cross-planks topped with two long planks set just far enough apart to support the tires of the vehicles that had once used them. But the past fifty years had taken their toll on the bridges. Chunks and hunks of the cross-planks had fallen away, leaving the water below them in plain sight. So at each bridge along the way, Mom and Dad, loaded down with fishing gear and food for the day, had no choice but to take our hands and pull us across to the other side, all the while telling us not to look down. While I have very few *snaps, scraps* or *snippets* to rely on here, the mere mention of 'Spring Lake' sends images drifting into my mind's camera.

The Bridges of Spring Lake

It was always an all-day fishing trip,
with all of the family trailing along,
following sandy paths or
making our own;
crossing rail-free bridges that spanned
drainage ditches where water
flowed freely beneath their rotting planks,
and where Mom and Dad had to
take our hands and drag us across
telling us all the while
not to look down.
By end of day,
the trek back to the car
was hotter, and seemed longer,
and we'd linger behind with Mom
to pick wild gooseberries
before running to catch up
so we wouldn't have to cross
those bridges alone.

Grandma's green thumbs were forever itching to dig up and take home a Spring Lake cactus. Little did I know at the time that I would someday (today, actually) be living on a Spring Lake sand hill; that I'd be fighting to rid my own back yard of the menacing cactus that Grandma always found so intriguing; and that images of painful thorns would stick in my mind's camera, demanding to be pulled out and developed.

The Thorn in Grandpa's *Back*side

The "talent" in my green thumb clings
to Grandma's knack for growing things.
For Grandma could replant or pot
a twig, or sprig, that most would not,
in her garden, or her living room,
And it would root, and thrive, and bloom.

But Grandma's thumb got out of hand
one day at Spring Lake, where the sand
grew thorns and thistles, in plain view,
on the trails to the fishing spot Dad knew;
though no one questioned how or why
the blooming cactus caught her eye,
or *when* she dug it, but she did,
with the two green thumbs she never hid;
but as the others trekked ahead,
she slipped back to the car instead;
and on a paper, on the seat,
she placed the cactus, flat, and neat.

Now when the fish had ceased to bite,
and bugs had moved in for the night,
the troop got to the car once more,
where Grandpa opened up the door
and jumped in on the very seat
where the cactus lay, all flat, and neat.

For days, then, Grandma had to look
on the weird position Grandpa took,
and work with tweezers, just to find
the thorns she'd put in his behind.
She'd've been much better off, she found,
had she left the cactus in the ground.

❖ Getting the Picture

Think back to a time when you or someone you know did something that turned out terribly wrong. From the images that form in your mind's camera, develop one or more word pictures describing the scene, using as many details as you can remember. Then use the word picture(s) to write a poem or an essay.

Discovering the World

When I met the man who would become my husband, I was surprised to find that his parents lived only a quarter of a mile from Spring Lake. Several years after we were married, we purchased their home place, atop a sand hill which, according to my husband, was "blown here over the years, from somewhere else." But equally as surprising has been the fact that the four girls I spent most of my Lincoln Elementary School recesses with, and with whom I later graduated high school, also moved to the Spring Lake area after they married. Four of us now live within a one-mile radius of each other, and a fifth lives just three miles away. So it was *not* surprising when memories of Lincoln School jumped into my mind's camera and played there, waiting to be developed.

Learning the Ropes

We were second-graders, five strong, and
all living within walking distance
of each other and the schoolyard,
so whoever arrived before the first bell
laid claim to the best sidewalk squares
for jacks or hopscotch or jump rope.

Then sidewalk squares gave way to
concrete steps, for "big girl" talk;
and different schools gave way to
different friends; and
different jobs gave way to
different worlds and different loves.
But, somehow, all those differences
brought us to the same town outside of town,
where we find ourselves once again
within walking distance of each other
and of schoolyard memories...

❖ Getting the Picture
Think back to your grade school days and how you spent your recesses. From the images that form in your mind's camera, develop one or more word pictures describing anything you remember about those recesses, including whatever games you played and who you played them with. Then use the word picture(s) to write a poem or an essay.

Building for the Future

With our entire back yard a potential sandbox, our son had little need for a manmade one. He spent most of every summer day digging and playing beneath the Chinese elm that shaded our kitchen window. And, when he was a little older, he'd set up a host of camouflaged army men — one of which now lives in his memory jar — that he'd ultimately blast with a battery of tiny firecrackers. But it was his softer side that bloomed into vivid images for my mind's camera.

No Special Day

I've been showered with flowers
On birthdays and such,
Given cards bearing greetings
With just the right touch;
But most precious of all came
On no special day:
Grubby hands held my first
Dandelion bouquet.
No big celebration,
No card to be read;
A simple, "Here, Mom,"
Was all that he said.

Years later, when he wanted to try out for his junior high track team, the sand road that runs alongside our property became his training field. As a result of his own hard work and persistent training, he set records in the 50 and 100 yard dashes (just prior to the switchover to meters), and won fifth place in the State finals. Yet today, images of those track 'n' field days race into my mind's camera.

The Sprinter

He stretches his legs and steps into the blocks
In the heat of the afternoon sun,
Then takes his position and nervously waits
For the crack of the starter's gun.
He leaps from the blocks, leans, and lengthens his stride,
For the uppermost thought in his mind
Is to build up more speed so he'll stay in the lead
And be first to the finish line.

❖ Getting the Picture

Help a young child pick a bouquet of dande-lions or violets for his mother or grand-mother. Note the way he holds the flowers; how he uses his hands and fingers; and the look of delight on his face when he hands over the flowers. Let the images that form in your mind's camera develop into one or more word pictures about the first bouquet *you* (truly or probably) picked for *your* mother. Then use the word picture(s) to write a poem or an essay.

Traipsing Through the Forest

Between our house and an open field to the west lie the leftovers of what was, in the '70s, a thriving Christmas tree farm. Trees whose branches were once shaped with saws and shears, and sprayed the appropriate Christmas-tree-green, now grow undisciplined and disheveled. Nevertheless, a glance in their direction still draws on the memories of the Christmas when we picked out a tree from our kitchen window, then walked through the snow to cut it down and drag it home; and of the Christmas a few years later when our son cut his own first tree from the remnants of that farm. That kitchen window still offers a view of leftover Christmas trees that bring family images into my mind's camera for quick developing.

Bringing in the Tree

For years our Christmas tree came from
The farm across the road.
Our son and both mixed labs would walk
Along to share the load.

But as our son reached college age,
He'd grumble and he'd fuss
Because we still expected him
To tag along with us.
And so we'd bicker back and forth,
Till he'd give in and say

He'd go, but that his presence couldn't
Matter anyway.

But then came graduation and
A home to call his own,
And early that December came
A call upon the phone:

Our son said, "Mom, I'm coming down
To find a Christmas tree;
Just wondered if you guys would want
To go along with me."

❖ Getting the Picture
Go to a Christmas tree farm, if possible, and observe a family choosing a tree to cut down, or just to buy. Listen to the excitement in their voices, and watch the expressions on their faces. From the images that form in your mind's camera, develop one or more word pictures about an old-fashioned Christmas, preferably one from your own childhood. Then use the word picture(s) to write a poem or an essay.

Playing Under the Sprinkler

With today's technology, and the constant use of fertilizers, herbicides, and irrigators, the sands of the Spring Lake area have become a goldmine for giant canneries. While our untreated hill supports a weak stand of grass that is continually threatened by sandburs, puncture weeds, and prickly pears, the fields surrounding us produce sizeable crops of seed corn, soybeans, popcorn, green beans, and pump-kins—all of which bring images tumbling into my mind's camera.

Harvesting the Giant's Beans

Stealthy as cats, they
paw their way through
the blackness, eyes glowing;
their incessant purring
drowning out even the crickets' lay,
while the thick green aroma of "fresh-cut"
filters through my screen.
Sometime in the night I think they've
curled up to sleep, but no, they've
only stopped to stretch before
resuming the hunt, intent on presenting
their prey to a jolly giant
who panics at the threat of rain.

From the time the spring rains stop till the crops are ready for harvest, we breathe the dust of plowing, planting, and cultivating, as well as the drifting mists sprayed by yellow biplanes.

My first encounter with a crop duster took place on a day when I was home alone. I stood frozen at the kitchen window as the small plane dipped over our line of trees and headed directly toward that window. I felt the sudden urge to move out of its way, yet I stood there, transfixed, looking in succession at its propeller, the bird-screen mesh behind it, and the black nothingness *behind that*.

Just as I thought the pilot might be joining me in my kitchen, the plane swooped up like a bird, showing its underbelly and the locked wheels that I thought for certain would clip the roof's edge. Once the images of it all had sifted and settled into my mind's camera, word pictures and a poem weren't far behind.

Crop Duster

Tempting fate—mine and his—
he targets the window
where I stand transfixed
by the blur of propeller and
bird-screen mesh
before he cuts abruptly up
giving me a bird's eye view
of underbelly and wheels
as they wind-brush
the shingles
of my roof.

Between crop dustings, giant irrigators on preset timers sweep the fields around our hill. Equipped with dozens of sprinkler heads working in *psht-psht-psht* half circles, and sprinkler arms working in *chk-a-chk-a-chk-a* sweeps, they cast millions of nitrogen-rich droplets on leaves that answer back with thankful *shu-shu-shu-shu-shu*s. Big as the irrigators are, their sounds take me back, to ice cold droplets of water twirled and hurled by the lawn sprinkler my sisters and I played under—usually in the sun, but once, and only once, in the dark of night.

Watered-Down Bargains

When summer days were long, and it
Was just too hot to play,
We'd put the sprinkler on the hose
And run beneath its spray.
And once, when Mom and Dad had all
Their yard work nearly done,
We coaxed them both to change their clothes
And join the slippery fun.
They both declined our offer, just
For fear of putting on
A side-show for the neighbors in
The center of our lawn;
Besides, they said we had to visit
Relatives, but when
We got back home they'd play beneath
The sprinkler with us then.

Well, it was long past midnight when
We got back, and we knew
That Mom and Dad thought we'd forgotten
What they'd said they'd do.
But kids don't oft' forget what parents
Offer up in trade,

So Mom and Dad were forced to keep
The bargain they had made.
We tip-toed 'neath the sprinkler with
A gasp in every breath
For, while the lawn got soaked again,
We nearly froze to death.
But Mom and Dad stuck with us through
Our every *splish* and *splat*—
And carefully avoided hasty
Bargains after that.

❖ Getting the Picture

If possible, go to a farming area where there is an irrigator in use, or set up a sprinkler in your own back yard. Listen to the difference in sounds coming from different sections of the irrigator/sprinkler, and to the sounds of the water falling on the leaves/grass. From the images that form in your mind's camera, develop one or more word pictures. Then use the word picture(s) to write a poem or an essay.

Chapter 8

Putting Time through a Sieve

Sieving the Ashes

*S*ieve. The word itself has a *smooth* and *oozing,* almost *flowing* sound. A touch-and-go trip through *The American Heritage Dictionary* shows that a *sieve* is a utensil used for "...sifting..."; that *sift* means "to put through a sieve...in order to separate the fine from the coarse"; and that *siftings* are the materials "removed or separated...with a sieve."

A sieve can be used in either of two ways: (1) for catching what we want to keep or (2) for catching what we intend to discard. Either way, something is saved, and something is thrown away or set aside for another use. Which it will be is ultimately up to the handler of the sieve.

Writers of all genres, who care to be published, are limited by maximum word, line, or page counts. That can mean cutting hundreds of words, or entire sections, stanzas, or stories that don't work. Nevertheless, most writers — especially poets — have to gather a wealth of information about their subject and then "put it all through a sieve" to separate the "fine" (the best) from the "coarse" (the less than best) in order to cut it down to the bare essentials.

Shortly after my husband and I purchased our rural property, we started dragging and hauling fruit tree prunings, and fallen twigs and branches from Chinese elms, to a convenient spot at the top of our orchard. That spot became a perpetual burn site that still sees the demise of old windows, doors, and lumber, all of which leave deposits of glass, hinges, and nails.

At first, we faithfully raked out the unburned materials and disposed of them. Then we gradually started leaving them to be burned on top of, time and again, occasionally shoveling the cold ashes onto a coarse screen that acts as a sieve. The clean potash that *sifted through* the screen was saved and scattered over our garden; shards of glass and metal *caught* by the screen were separated, the glass to be discarded, the metal set aside and sold as scrap. So it is with recording, and then sifting through, written details. Some are worth saving, like the metal; some sift on through to be saved for elsewhere, like the potash; and some simply need to be discarded, like the glass.

When I decided to record my memoirs in the form of poems that readers can "step into" and relate to their own memories, I was painfully aware of the fact that a poem can only hold so many details; that a book can only hold so many poems; and that only the people involved in a particular facet of my life would care to read every detail of it anyway. Hence the need for putting time through a sieve, for picking and choosing what thoughts and memories should or should not be included in a poem and, ultimately, what poems should or should not be included in a scrapbook or memoir.

Taking Charge of the Sieve

The sands of time have a way of burying and preserving our memories. While some remain unscathed, and just need to be uncovered, some get scattered and broken and have to be sought out and gathered up.

Most of the blow sand that has been brought to our hill through the ages has stayed, not only to form and shape the hill, but also to bury and hoard its own stockpile of history. Effortlessly making its way through and under cracks and crevices of old machine sheds, it sifts and drifts over lumber, tools, and other stored items, the most fascinating of which was a six-pack of vintage 7*Up* bottles that we uncovered by accident. All six bottles *and* their carton were unscathed, but for the dust. Outside the sheds, however, where the unprotected sands of our driveway get washed and pounded by summer rains, pieces of the hill's past continue to surface, as if time itself is holding the sieve.

Time Sieves the Hill

Time sieves the hill
for remnants of itself
as summer rains
rinse grains of sand
no longer shifted by the wind,
coaxing them to give up
shards of pottery and glass,
bottles and toys,
blue granite dippers and
square nails,
all buried on purpose or
by chance—
time sieves the hill
for remnants of itself.

Unfortunately, waiting for time to sift through our memories for us may leave us with little time in which to record them. So, instead of sitting back and waiting for time to do the sifting, I have chosen to grab my shovel and dig up enough *snaps*, *scraps* and *snippets* to put through my own sieve. And I invite you here and now to sharpen your pick, polish your shovel, and start digging and sieving the seemingly lost treasures that are a part of your past. In fact, I encourage anyone who has even a *single* memory to share with a child or grandchild, niece or nephew, to write it down now, in any shape or form.

However you view the sieve — for catching what's important *or* for discarding what isn't — use it to the best of your ability. As the handler of my own sieve, my motto is to *catch what's important; throw away only what is absolutely meaningless; and set the siftings aside for another day.*

❖ Getting the Picture
Go back to any previous *Getting the Picture* exercise that you had trouble with — one where your mind's camera gave you so faint an image that you couldn't develop it into a word picture. Then begin an uninterrupted session of *guided* freewriting (see Part I, Chapter 3), writing nonstop and channeling all of your thoughts to the person, event, or item you wish to describe. From whatever clear images appear during your freewriting session, develop one or more word pictures. Then use the word picture(s) to write a poem or an essay.

Part III

Using a Wide-Angle Lens

Chapter 1

Moving Toward the Window

Looking Past *the Window*

Windows are contradictory necessities, simultaneously offering false security and false freedom — false security because few of them can keep us safe from anything or anyone determined to get past them or through them; false freedom because they allow us to see, and long for, what lies beyond them while keeping us from touching or experiencing whatever that may be.

    For thirteen years, my older sisters and I shared a corner room that had two windows, one on each outside wall; a walk-in closet; and one-and-a-half beds that Mom rearranged every spring and fall. After one such spring rearranging, I ended up with the side of the double bed that was shoved into a corner so that the foot of the bed was right under a window.

That summer, Dad also bought a heavy-duty, reversible window fan for the middle room of our house and cleverly used it to exhaust the hot air from the entire house by drawing air through slightly opened windows in other rooms. Most nights, while my sisters slept, I chose to lie at the foot of the bed, directly under the window, where I could look at the moon and stars while the artificial breeze swept over me. It was from that window that I saw the sky turn red the night of Pekin's historic distillery fire and, again, the night a north side barn burned to the ground.

My fascination with windows was further fueled by a storybook train trip through the Scottish countryside with my parents, in 1957. From the window of our private compartment, the scenery was whizzing by all too quickly for me. So I stepped out into the narrow corridor, where the conductor had slid the upper halves of the windows down. I spent the rest of the trip standing at one of those open windows, watching to see what was coming up along the way.

The smells of coal and soot from the quaint steam engine complemented the view, but it didn't do much for my appearance. By the time we arrived at our destination, I was sporting a charcoal mask, and my hair was heavy with soot. I needed only to turn to

another detailed travel journal to find images
that chugged their way into my mind's camera.

Live Training on Track

September 1957: England to Scotland
Three first class "sleepers":
two connected, but a single for me;
all 4 x 6s with 30-inch beds;
windows with pull-down shades;
a small sink in one corner;
and a chamber pot on the floor.

Through the night, I ponder to the rumble
of wheels on steel and voices of passengers
boarding and alighting
at each stop along the way.

Morning brings the challenge of
donning nylon stockings to the
rock and sway of the car
and the self-embarrassment of
kicking over the chamber pot.

We meet for breakfast in
a private compartment with facing seats,
but the corridor is more inviting,
with upper windows slid down enough
to accommodate my head as I
crane my neck to keep sight of the engine
that pulls us smoothly around curves,
belching sulfur and soot in gray-black style,
and graciously applying
a charcoal mask to all but my eyes.

Only months before, an apartment in Düsseldorf, Germany, offered a bay-type window that overlooked our drab street and the other buildings on the block. Opened, the windows relieved smells of musty tapestries and damp plaster, but they also brought the sound of horses' hooves clippity-clopping along the cobblestone street and the call of the produce man shouting "Kartoffeln!" from the curb below.

But even more tantalizing for me were French doors that opened off my parents' bedroom, onto a very small balcony that faced the backs of red brick buildings and downspouts and overlooked community clotheslines.

I spent sunny days on that balcony, writing letters to my school friends back home, but also writing highly detailed word pictures of our furnished apartment, right down to the contents of its kitchen cupboards and the smell of its plaster and wallpaper. Those word pictures, with few additions or subtractions, became a lengthy poem describing the apartment I didn't want to forget.

The Time Capsule

June 1957: Düsseldorf, Germany
"Feldstrasse Drie und Swanzig A":
the extent of our German, and
all that distinguishes

our three-month dwelling
from run-on blocks of mustard-brown stucco
that narrowly escaped the bombings
of World War II.

Beyond the numbers, the stairwell reeks
of bitter cold tenants
who scatter like rodents
to pull back yellowed lace curtains,
buzz the door open when we ring,
and count our footsteps
on the concrete stairs.

Every turning of our key unleashes
pent-up fumes of repeated-damp plaster
and wallpaper paste
mingled with the stuffiness
of prewar tapestries and the aging wood
of sturdy, locked hutches that hoard
fine china candlesticks, clocks and vases,
three sizes of silverware, and
three dozen miniature glasses.

A square wooden clock that is
surely as old as I imagine its owner to be
greets us with an irregular *tick!*
where its pendulum *sticks!*
and the weightless end of its chain
swoops up
to a nail in the wall.

Kitchen cupboards
overflowing with pots and pans,
and those reserved for bottles and brushes
and halves and handles

of white china cups and saucers
(that can't be repaired but
can't be parted with either),
can only be contained
by locking their doors.

From dining room windows that crank out
over Feldstrasse,
we will learn to pitch coins
to strolling minstrels;
toss a red net bag to the peddler who
weighs and delivers kartoffeln to our door;
watch street sweepers broom their way along
streets, and garbage collectors
descend beneath sidewalks by way
of electric lifts;
pay the chimney sweep who comes to our door
in stovepipe hat and covered in soot
from head to foot;
and determine the time of day
by the *tick-tock, clip-clop*
of Clydesdales from the brewery
around the corner and up the street.

And, rain or shine, I will yield
to the compelling allurement
of a scant balcony
that faces red brick walls and
three-story downspouts;
where hinges of a table
built to collapse against its outer wall
have long since rusted in the *up* position;
where narrow wooden doors and
a hint of whitewash hold back
the kinds of things I imagine

old German ladies tend to save:
an ironing board minus its legs,
a rusting tin can,
two slivers of rotting wood,
a canvas bag,
and a wooden contraption
for drying clothes;
where frayed cotton cord
wound round the pipe stand
of a faded umbrella
holds in place the decaying remains
of a flower box that lets mud drizzle through
to laundry strung out on the balcony below;
and where I, in turn, survive
sporadic showerings
of tablecloth crumbs
and bird cage cleanings.

November of 1957 found my parents and me living in Australia, about twenty-one kilometers north and a little west of Melbourne (between the then small villages of Tullamarine and Broadmeadows). Despite the panoramic view offered by ceiling-to-floor windows in our living room, it was the rectangular-shaped stationary window above our breakfast nook that held my attention on school days, when morning rains more often than not set the rhythm of my fountain pen as I completed my homework at 5:00 a.m., before my parents got up and my dad headed off to work. While I couldn't see through the darkness beyond the window, I could see the rain that the window was holding out. More word pictures for my journal.

In the '70s, another train ride, this time to Toronto, Canada, with my husband, inspired my writing soul. In our sleeping compartment, I chose to sleep next to the window, which I kept open all night long. Every time the train pulled into a station along the way, I lifted the shade just enough to take in the activities and the enthusiasm or boredom of passengers on the platform.

My true understanding of windows, though, was summed up one day while I was entertaining our baby granddaughter in the back seat of our car. Our favorite naptime book was *Goodnight Moon* (the brilliantly simple book by Margaret Wise, published by Brown, Harper & Row), and I was trying desperately to get her to *see* the moon, which was still visible in the morning sky. But all she could see was a fly on the *inside* of the window. I acknowledged to her that, yes, indeed, there was a fly, but kept pointing at the moon *on the other side* of the window. A look of sheer delight came over her face when she finally looked *past* the fly, and *past* the window, and saw the moon.

As poets and writers who desire to write about our pasts, we have to learn to look *through* and *past* the windows, at whatever lies beyond them, even if it appears that what's out there is beyond our reach. If the windows can't readily be opened, we can still take advantage of the freedoms they offer in letting us see, or imagine, what lies beyond them. In doing so, we learn how to "open" those windows and take in the touch, sounds, and smells that enhance whatever images form in our minds' cameras.

Chapter 2

Putting the Past in Perspective

Dwelling In, Not On, the Past

During the two years I lived in Australia with my parents, I kept a highly-detailed diary of our daily events and experiences. Even as a teenager, I scribbled notes on whatever I could find at the time, be it napkins, envelopes, or cash register receipts, and ended up with a conglomeration of dated paragraphs and phrases that I was still translating, sorting, and typing up, first on a manual typewriter, then on an electric one, when we got back home. When the diary was finally done, I set it aside on a closet shelf. Then came the computer and the nagging realization that pictures and documents would greatly enhance the book.

For several years, I weighed the advantages with the obvious. It would be a time-consuming job, but I could find the time,

I was sure. It would require patience and determination, but I had plenty of both. It wasn't something that had to be done, but I wanted to do it. All things considered, I couldn't rest until I had put together a 500 page book: *The South Wind Blows Cold (Down Under)*, complete with photographs *(snaps)*, scanned documents I had saved throughout the trip *(scraps)*, and details I was determined not to forget *(snippets)*.

It didn't matter that no one except for my poor husband, who graciously proofread every word of it for me, would ever read it or even want to. What did matter was that once it was done, and once I had that part of my life documented, I could, in a sense, let it go.

While some of us live to write about the past, some, for one reason or another, are adamant about leaving it right where it is—behind them.

Shadows of the Past

One day I turned my TV on
And heard a woman say,
"Today is all that matters; I've
No need for yesterday."
She said her son is fully grown
And doesn't mind at all
That there is not one baby picture
"Cluttering" her wall.
What's more, she said she does not save
What "reeks of days gone by"

And has no use for sentiments
That keepsakes signify.

I felt a twinge of sadness for
The woman *and* her son,
For them to think the past can be
Ignored by anyone.
I'd rather know that I can walk
The roads where time has led,
To reminisce, through memories
That linger in its stead
And cherish *any* relics that
Remind me of the past
As, day by day, I live beneath
The shadows that they cast.

Whether we like it or not, we are all products of our pasts. While it isn't always healthy to dwell *on* the past, it is sometimes necessary to dwell *in* it, just long enough to record it. Once done, it can be put in its rightful place — behind us.

❖ Getting the Picture
Go to a window, preferably one *without* a beautiful view. One facing an alley, or one that's being peppered with raindrops, could very well be the one that offers the most inspiration. Open the window, if possible. If not, make sure you look *past* the window pane. Let the images that form in your mind's camera develop into one or more word pictures describing the sights, sounds and smells (real or imagined)

that lie beyond that window. Then use the word picture(s) to write a poem or an essay.

Conclusion

Getting to the End of the Roll

The Brownie camera with which I became an amateur photographer at the age of nine used size 127 film that offered a mere eight exposures per roll. As a result, I learned to view getting to the end of the roll in two different ways. If I still had a few moments in time to capture, I dreaded seeing the number 8 come up in the little red window. If, on the other hand, I thought that one exposure inside that camera might be a prizewinner, then the end of the roll couldn't come soon enough.

I've learned to view reading in much the same way. If a book offers *anything* in the way of helping me to become a better writer, its final chapter always comes too soon. But if it offers more — if it inspires me to want to set it aside and actually get down to writing — then the final chapter can't come soon enough. However you view this book, my hope is that it has helped and/or inspired you in some small way.

By now, your *Getting the Picture* binder should contain at least a few of the poems or essays suggested, or inspired, by the exercises. Hopefully, along the way, you've gathered some *snaps*, *scraps* and *snippets* of your own and have even veered off the path a little and found other tools that haven't been dealt with here. If so, you undoubtedly have a good start for a meaningful journal, as well as for a treasured scrapbook or memoir. If that's the case, then I have met my goal in writing this book. And with that, I wish you many hours of happy hunting.

www.ingramcontent.com/pod-product-compliance
Lightning Source LLC
Chambersburg PA
CBHW021946290426
44108CB00012B/975